Dear Roger,

Step aside, sometimes, and rest
your eyes on these pages,
the visions they reflect.

I hope you find Refreshment
here, as I have.

my love,

Edie

The Longing for Home

Other Books by Frederick Buechner

FREDERICK BUECHNER

◆ ◆ ◆ ◆ ◆

THE LONGING
FOR HOME

Recollections and Reflections

HarperSanFrancisco
An Imprint of HarperCollins*Publishers*

HarperCollins Web Site: http://www.harpercollins.com
HarperCollins® ▄▇® and HarperSanFrancisco™
are trademarks of HarperCollins Publishers, Inc.

FIRST EDITION

Library of Congress Cataloging-in-Publication Data

Buechner, Frederick.
    The longing for home : recollections and reflections / Frederick Buechner.
        p. cm.
    ISBN 0-06-061191-X (cloth)
    1. Buechner, Frederick.—Homes and haunts. 2. Novelists, American—20th century—Biography. 3. Pittsburgh (Pa.)—Social life and customs. 4. Buechner, Frederick.—Religion. 5. Presbyterian Church—Clergy—Biography. 6. Clergy—United States—Biography. I. Title.
PS3552.U35Z463   1996
813'.54—dc20   96–1008

96 97 98 99 00 ❖ RRDH 10 9 8 7 6 5 4 3 2

For my grandsons
Oliver, Dylan, Benjamin, Tristan,
and Brendan

◊　　◊　　◊　　◊　　◊

Contents

◇ ◇ ◇ ◇ ◇

The Longing for Home

◇　◇　◇　◇　◇

Introduction

The words *time* and *tide* trace their ancestry back to a common Indo-European root, and part of what they still have in common after going their separate ways all these years is the sense of ebbing and flowing. Time, like the receding waters of the ocean, bears all of us who are time's children farther and farther away from the near shore and closer and closer to those mysterious depths where we will come finally to our time's end.

When I was young, I knew that perfectly well, but I lived as though my time was endless. When I was in my fifties and early sixties even, I deluded myself with the fantasy that I was still somehow middle-aged and had roughly as much time left to live as I had lived already, which seemed endless enough for all practical purposes. But now that I find myself pushing seventy hard, I have finally begun to wise up. It is no longer just in my mind that I know I am rather a good deal closer to the end of my time than I am to its beginning. I know it in my stomach, and there is a lot of

1

sadness in knowing it. But that is by no means all there is. Who would want it to be day forever and never night, after all? Who would choose to be awake forever and never get a chance to sleep?

But the tide that carries us farther and farther away from our beginning in time is also the tide that turns and carries us back again. In other words, it is true what they say: the older we grow, the more we find ourselves returning to the days when we were young. More vividly than ever before, I think, we find ourselves remembering the one particular house that was our childhood home. We remember the books we read there. We remember the people we loved there. The first group of pieces in this collection has to do with home in that sense—the home we knew and will always long for, be homesick for.

The author of the Letter to the Hebrews, after listing some of the great heroes of Scripture, writes, "These all died in faith, not having received what was promised, but having seen it and greeted it from afar, and having acknowledged that they were strangers and exiles on the earth. For people who speak thus make it clear that they are seeking a homeland" (11:13–14). One way or another the second group of pieces has to do with home in that sense—the home we dream of finding and for which we also long. Because I believe that it is by Grace that we set out on our search for it and that it is Faith and Hope that keep us searching, I have added at the end of that group short pieces on the three of them aimed particularly at men and women who every Sunday face the task of somehow showing forth from the pulpit that these are not just theological ideas but are as real as they, the preachers, themselves are real, which it is crucial that they somehow also show forth. And, of course, the last piece of all is about the One who is himself our true and final home. "That he may dwell in us and we in him," is the way the old prayer puts it.

What is the connection between the home we knew and the home we dream? I believe that what we long for most in the home we knew is the peace and charity that, if we were lucky, we first came to experience there, and I believe that it is that same peace and charity we dream of finding once again in the home that the tide of time draws us toward. The first home foreshadows the final home, and the final home hallows and fulfills what was most precious in the first. That, at least, is my prayer for all of us. And that is what these pages are all about.

Part 1

◆　◆　◆　◆

THE HOME
WE KNEW

1

◊   ◊   ◊   ◊   ◊

The Longing for Home

H ome sweet home. There's no place like home. Home is where
you hang your hat, or, as a waggish friend of mine once
said, Home is where you hang yourself. "Home is the sailor,
home from sea, / And the hunter home from the hill." What the
word *home* brings to mind before anything else, I believe, is a
place, and in its fullest sense not just the place where you happen
to be living at the time, but a very special place with very special at-
tributes which make it clearly distinguishable from all other places.
The word *home* summons up a place—more specifically a house
within that place—which you have rich and complex feelings
about, a place where you feel, or did feel once, uniquely *at home*,
which is to say a place where you feel you belong and which in
some sense belongs to you, a place where you feel that all is some-
how ultimately well even if things aren't going all that well at any
given moment. To think about home eventually leads you to think
back to your childhood home, the place where your life started, the

place which off and on throughout your life you keep going back to if only in dreams and memories and which is apt to determine the kind of place, perhaps a place inside yourself, that you spend the rest of your life searching for even if you are not aware that you are searching. I suspect that those who as children never had such a place in actuality had instead some kind of dream of such a home, which for them played an equally crucial part.

I was born in 1926 and therefore most of my childhood took place during the years of the Great Depression of the thirties. As economic considerations kept my father continually moving from job to job, we as a family kept moving from place to place with the result that none of the many houses we lived in ever became home for me in the sense I have described. But there was one house which did become home for me in that sense and which for many years after the last time I saw it in 1938 or so I used to dream about and which I still often think about although by now I am old enough to be the grandfather of the small boy I was when I first knew it.

It was a large white clapboard house that belonged to my maternal grandparents and was located in a suburb of Pittsburgh, Pennsylvania, called East Liberty, more specifically in a private residential enclave in East Liberty called Woodland Road which had a uniformed guard at the gate who checked you in and out to make sure you had good reason for being there. For about twenty years or so before he went more or less broke and moved away in his seventies with my grandmother to live out the rest of their days in North Carolina, my grandfather was a rich man and his house was a rich man's house, as were all the others in Woodland Road, including the one that belonged to Andrew Mellon, who lived nearby. It was built on a hill with a steep curving driveway and surrounded by green lawns and horse chestnut trees, which put out white blossoms in May and unbelievably sticky buds that my younger brother and I used to stir up with leaves and twigs in a sweetgrass basket, calling it witches' brew. It also produced glistening brown buckeyes that you had to split off the tough, thorny husks to find and could make tiny chairs out of with pins for legs or attach to a string and hurl into the air or crack other people's buckeyes with to see which would hold out the longest.

The house itself had a full-length brick terrace in front and lots of French windows on the ground floor and bay windows above and dormers on the third floor with a screened-in sleeping porch in the back under which was the kitchen porch, which had a zinc-lined, pre-electric icebox on it that the iceman delivered ice to and whose musty, cavelike smell I can smell to this day if I put my mind to it. To the right of the long entrance hall was the library lined with glassed-in shelves and books, some of which I can still remember like the slim, folio-sized picture books about French history with intricate full-page color plates by the great French illustrator Job, and my great-grandfather Golay's set of the works of Charles Dickens bound in calf like law books with his name stamped on the front cover. To the left of the hall was the living room, which I remember best for a horsehair settee covered in cherry red damask that was very uncomfortable and prickly to sit on and a Chinese vase almost large enough for a boy my size to hide in, and an English portrait done in the 1840s of a little girl named Lavinia Holt, who is wearing a dress of dotted white organdy with a slate blue sash and is holding in her left hand, her arm almost fully extended to the side, a spidery, pinkish flower that might be honeysuckle. In the basement there was a billiard room with a green baize table, which as far as I know was never used by anybody and a moosehead mounted on the wall that my brother and I and our cousin David Wick used to pretend to worship for reasons I have long since forgotten as the God of the Dirty Spittoon and several tall bookcases full of yellow, paper-bound French novels that ladies of the French Alliance, of which my half French-Swiss grandmother was a leading light, used to come and borrow from time to time.

At the end of the entrance hall a broad white staircase ascended to a landing with a bench on it and then turned the corner and went up to the second floor where the grown-ups' bedrooms were, including my grandparents', which had a bay window and a sun-drenched window seat where I used to count the pennies I emptied out of a little penny bank of my grandmother's made like the steel helmet of a World War I French *poilu*. The stairway then continued on up to the third floor, where you could look down through the banister railing to the carpeted hall, which seemed a dizzying distance below. The third floor was the part of the house that for many years I used to go back to in my dreams. My brother's and my bedroom was there, with a little gas fire that on winter mornings Ellen, the maid, used to light for us before we got out of bed, and the servants' rooms, and other rooms full of humpbacked trunks covered with steamship labels and tied-up cardboard boxes and round Parisian hatboxes and all sorts of other treasures my brother and I never fully explored—which is perhaps why for all those years my dreams kept taking me back for another look. The smell of the house that I remember best was the smell of cooking applesauce. Out in the kitchen paneled with dark matchboard, Williams, the cook, put cinnamon in it for flavoring, and the fragrance as it simmered and steamed on top of the stove was warm and blurred and dimly pungent and seemed somehow full of enormous comfort and kindness.

What was there about that house that made it home in a way that all the other houses of my childhood never even came close to being? The permanence of it was part of the answer—the sense I had that whereas the other houses came and went, this one was there always and would go on being there for as far into the future as I could imagine, with Ellen bringing my grandmother her glass of buttermilk on a silver tray just at eleven every morning, and my grandfather going off to his downtown office and returning in time for a cocktail before dinner with the evening paper under his arm and maybe something he'd bought at the bakery on the way home, and the Saturday night suppers when the cook was out and the menu, in honor of the New England half of my grandmother's background, was always mahogany-colored beans baked with salt pork and molasses, steamed Boston brown bread with raisins in it, and strong black coffee boiled in a pot with an eggshell to settle the grounds and sweetened with lumps of sugar and cream heavy enough to whip.

And beauty was another part of the answer, beauty that I took in through my pores almost before I so much as knew the word *beauty*—the paintings and books and green lawns, the thunder of water falling in a long, silver braid from the gooseneck spigot into the pantry sink, the lighting of lamps with their fringed shades at dusk, the knee-length silk mandarin's coat with a coral lining and flowers and birds embroidered all over it that my grandmother sometimes wore in the evenings, and out behind the house by the grassed-over tennis court the white stables that were used to garage, among other cars, the elegant old Marmon upholstered in salmon-colored leather that had belonged to my mother in her flapper days and hadn't been used since.

But more than all of these things that made that house home, or at the heart of all those things, was my grandmother, whom for reasons lost to history I called Naya. How to evoke her? She loved books and music and the French language of her father, who had emigrated from Geneva to fight on the Union side in the Civil War and eventually died of a shoulder wound he received from a sniper's bullet at the siege of Petersburg. She loved Chesterfield cigarettes and the novels of Jean Ingelow and a daiquiri before dinner and crossword puzzles and she spoke the English language with a wit and eloquence and style that I have never heard surpassed. She loved to talk about the past as much as I loved to listen to her bring it to life with her marvelous, Dickensian descriptions, and when she talked about the present, she made it seem like a richly entertaining play which we both of us had leading roles in and at the same time were watching unfold from the safety and comfort of our seats side by side in the dress circle. The love she had for me was not born of desperate need for me like my mother's love, but had more to do simply with her interest in me as a person and with the pleasure she took in my interest in her as the one grandchild she had who was bookish the way she was and who sat endlessly enraptured by the spells she cast.

On my thirty-fourth birthday, when she was going on ninety-one, she wrote me a letter in which she said, "[this] is to wish you many and many a happy year to come. And to wish for you that along the way you may meet someone who will be to you the delight you have been to me. By which I mean someone of a younger generation." For all its other glories, the house on Woodland Road could never have become home without the extraordinary delight to me of her presence in it and the profound sense of serenity and well-being that her presence generated, which leads me to believe that if, as I started by saying, the first thing the word *home* brings to mind is a place, then the next and perhaps most crucial thing is people and maybe ultimately a single person.

Can it really, that home on Woodland Road, have been as wonderful as I make it sound, at least to myself, or has my memory reshaped it? The answer is that yes, of course, it was every bit that wonderful, and probably even more so in ways I have omitted from this account, and that is precisely why my memory has never let go of it as it has let go of so much else, but has continually reshaped it, the way the waves of the sea are continually reshaping the shimmering cliff, until anything scary and jagged is worn away, with the result that what has principally survived is a sense—how to put it right?—of charity and justice and order and peace that I have longed to find again ever since and have longed to establish inside myself.

All of this makes me wonder about the home that my wife and I created for ourselves and our three daughters, both of us coming from the homes of our childhood and consciously or unconsciously drawing on those memories as we went about making a new home for the family that we were becoming. For thirty-odd years the five of us lived in the same house, at first just during vacations but eventually all year round, so that there was never any question as to where home was. It was a much smaller white clapboard house than my grandparents', but it was built on a much higher hill and surrounded not so much by lawns as by the meadows, pastures, and woods of our corner of southern Vermont. The house had a number of small bedrooms in it with a smallish, rather narrow living room, which all the other rooms more or less opened into, so that to sit there was to be aware of pretty much everything that was going on under our roof. For me as the ever watchful and ever anxious father, this had the advantage or disadvantage of letting me keep an eye on my children's comings and goings without, I hoped, giving them the sense that I was perpetually keeping tabs on them. But as they began to get bigger and noisier, there were times when I yearned for a place to escape to once in a while, so we built on a wing with a large living room paneled in the silvery gray siding of a couple of tumbledown prerevolutionary barns. I don't think that it was in conscious emulation of the Woodland Road library that I filled the new room with shelves full of wonderful books—a few of them copies of some of the same ones that Naya had had, like the Job-illustrated French histories—but I'm sure that the memory of it was in the back of my mind somewhere. Like Naya, and almost certainly because of her, I was fascinated by the past of my family— the mid-nineteenth-century German immigrants on my father's side and the mixture of English, French, Pennsylvania Dutch, old New England, and almost everything else on my mother's—and I became in a way the family archivist, the keeper of the family graves, and collected in the cupboards beneath the bookshelves as many old photograph albums, documents, letters, genealogies, and assorted family memorabilia as little by little came my way through various relatives who knew of my interest and sent them to me. It was in that silvery gray room too that for some twenty years I both read my books and wrote them. It was there that I listened to music and to what I could hear of the longings and fears and lusts and holiness of my own life. It was in that room that our best Christmases took place, with a nine-foot tree that we would all go out together and cut down in the woods and then trim with decorations of our own making.

What my wife brought to the home we were creating was entirely different. The chief delight of her childhood in New Jersey had been not indoor things, as with me, but outdoor things. She had loved horses and animals of all kinds and growing things in gardens and almost by nature knew as much about trees and birds and flowers as most people have to learn from books and then struggle to remember. She planted a fifty-by-hundred-foot vegetable garden and flowers all over the place. She saw to it that each of our children had not only horses to ride but other animals to love and take care of—for Sharmy, Aracana chickens, who laid eggs of three different colors; for Dinah, a pig who grew to the size of a large refrigerator and didn't suffer fools gladly; and for Katherine, some fawn-colored Toggenberg goats who skittered around the barnyard dropping their berries and gazing out at the hills through the inscrutable slits of their eyes.

Like everybody else, what we furnished home with was ourselves, in other words. We furnished it with the best that we knew and the best that we were, and we furnished it also with everything that we were not wise enough to know and the shadow side of who we were as well as the best side, because we were not self-aware enough to recognize those shadows and somehow both to learn from them and to disempower them.

It became home for us in a very full sense. It was the place where we did the best we knew how to do as father and mother and as wife and husband. It was the little world we created to be as safe as we knew how to make it for ourselves and for our children from the great world outside, which I more than my wife was afraid of especially for our children's sake because I remembered so vividly the dark and dangerous times of my own childhood, which were very much part of me still and continue to be. In that Vermont house I found refuge from the dark, as I always had, mainly in books, which, unlike people, can always be depended upon to tell the same stories in the same way and are always there when you need them and can always be set aside when you need them no longer. I believe my wife would say that her refuge from the dark has always been the world of animals and growing things.

Did this home we made become for our children as richly home as my grandparents' home had been for me as a child? How would they answer that question if I were ever brave enough to ask it? Did I hold them too close with my supervigilance? Did my wife perhaps not hold them close enough? Were our lives in deep country away from any easy access to town or neighbors too intense and isolated for our own good? Did they find in our house on the hill anything like the same sense of charity, justice, order, and peace that I had found on Woodland Road? As they grow older, will they draw upon what was best about it as they make homes of their own with their husbands and children? I don't know any of these answers. Maybe they themselves don't entirely know them. Maybe even in their early thirties they are still too close to their childhood to be able to see it with the detachment with which I see mine in my late sixties. It was almost not until I found myself putting these thoughts together that I fully realized that my own true home had not been any of the places my brother and I had lived both before and after our father's suicide when I was ten years old, not even the places where we were happiest, but had been instead that house in

East Liberty, where we never really lived in any permanent sense but only visited. Will our children remember the house in Vermont as their true home? Or are the words *true home* perhaps too much to apply to even the happiest home that lies within our power to create? Are they words that always point to a reality beyond themselves?

In a novel called *Treasure Hunt*, which I wrote some years ago, there is a scene of homecoming. The narrator, a young man named Antonio Parr, has been away for some weeks and on his return finds that his small son and some other children have made a sign for him that reads WELCOME HONE with the last little leg of the *m* in *home* missing so that it turns it into an *n*. "It seemed oddly fitting," Antonio Parr says when he first sees it. "It was good to get home, but it was home with something missing or out of whack about it. It wasn't much, to be sure, just some minor stroke or serif, but even a minor stroke can make a major difference." And then a little while later he remembers it a second time and goes on to add "WELCOME HONE, the sign said, and I can't help thinking again of Gideon and Barak, of Samson and David and all the rest of the crowd. . . who, because some small but crucial thing was missing, kept looking for it come hell or high water wherever they went till their eyes were dim and their arches fallen. . . . In the long run I suppose it would be to think of everybody if you knew enough about them to think straight" ("Treasure Hunt," in *The Book of Bebb* [San Francisco: HarperCollins, 1990], p. 529). The reference, of course, is to the eleventh chapter of the Letter to the Hebrews, where, after listing some of the great heroes and heroines of biblical faith, the author writes, "These all died in faith, not having received what was promised, but having seen it and greeted it from afar, and having acknowledged that they were strangers and exiles on the earth. For people who speak thus make it clear that they are seeking a homeland" (vv. 13–14).

If we are lucky, we are born into a home, or like me find a home somewhere else along the way during childhood, or, failing that, at least, one hopes, find some good dream of a home. And, if our luck holds, when we grow up, we make another home for ourselves and for our family if we get married and acquire one. It is the place of all places that we feel most at home in, most at peace and most at one in, and as I sketched out in my mind that scene in my novel, I thought of it primarily as a scene that would show Antonio Parr's great joy at returning to his home after such a long absence. But then out of nowhere, and entirely unforeseen by me, there came into my mind that sign with the missing leg of the *m*. I hadn't planned to have it read *hone* instead of *home*. It was in no sense a novelistic device I'd contrived. It's simply the way I saw it. From as deep a place within me as my books and my dreams come from, there came along with the misspelled sign this revelation that although Antonio Parr was enormously glad to be at home at last, he recognized that there was something small but crucial missing, which if only for a moment made him feel, like Gideon and Barak before him, that he was in some sense a stranger and an exile there. It is when he comes home that he recognizes most poignantly that he is, at a deep level of his being, homeless, and that whatever it is that is missing, he will spend the rest of his days longing for it and seeking to find it.

The word *longing* comes from the same root as the word *long* in the sense of length in either time or space and also the word *belong*, so that in its full richness *to long* suggests to yearn for a long time for something that is a long way off and something that we feel we belong to and that belongs to us. The longing for home is so universal a form of longing that there is even a special word for it, which is of course homesickness, and what I have been dealing with so far is that form of homesickness known as nostalgia or longing for the past as home. Almost all of the photographs that I have managed to find of my grandparents' house in Pittsburgh show simply the house itself. There is a view from the front with the long brick terrace and the French windows, and another from the rear with the sleeping porch over the kitchen porch beneath it and the bay window of my grandparents' bedroom and the tall, arched window on the first landing of the central staircase. There is an interior shot of the living room with Lavinia Holt gazing out over the grand piano, which has a fringed shawl draped over it and which, as far as I can remember, Naya was the only one of us ever to use, picking out tunes with one finger every once and so often because that was as near as she ever came to knowing how to play it, and another shot shows the library with the wicker peacock chair at one side of the fireplace and the white sofa at the far end where Naya used to let me help her do the Sunday crossword puzzle. But there is one photograph that has a person in it, and the person is Naya herself.

It is winter and there has been a thaw. Wet snow clings to the bare branches of the trees, and the air is full of mist. Naya is standing on the front terrace in profile. She is looking pensively out toward the lawn. She is wearing a short fur jacket and a fur hat with her hands in the jacket pockets. She has on galoshes or arctics as they were called in those days. The terrace is covered with snow except in the foreground where it has melted away in patches, and you can see her reflection in the wet brick. When I look at that photograph I can almost literally feel the chill air of Pittsburgh on that winter day in 1934 or whenever it was and smell wet fur and wet wool mittens and hear the chink of arctics when you walk in them without doing the metal fasteners all the way up. I can almost literally feel in my stomach my eight-year-old excitement at having the ground deep in snow and at being in that marvelous house and at Naya's being there. If it's true that you can't go home again, it is especially true when the home in question has long since gone and been replaced by another and when virtually all the people who used to live there have long since gone too and are totally beyond replacing. But sometimes I can almost believe that if I only knew the trick of it, I could actually go back anyway, that just some one small further movement of memory or will would be enough to transport me to that snowy terrace again where Naya would turn to me in her fur jacket and would open the front door with her gloved hand and we would enter the cinnamon, lamp-lit dusk of the house together. But it is a trick that I have never quite mastered, and for that reason I have to accept my homesickness as chronic and incurable.

The house in Vermont, on the other hand, is still very much there, but about seven years ago we moved out of it into what used to be my wife's parents' house down the hill a few hundred yards so that now it has returned to being the guest house that it originally was before we became the permanent guests. Our children still use it from time to time, but I don't go back to it very often myself. Not long after we moved out, I remember apologizing to it for that. The house was empty except for me, and I stood in the living room and told it out loud not to be upset that we don't live there anymore and rarely return to visit. I said it must never think that it failed us in any way. I told it what wonderful years we had had there and how happy we'd been and tried to explain that we would always remember it with great gratitude and affection, all of which is true. But what keeps me from going back except on rare occasions is that it is so full of emptiness now—the children's rooms still littered with their stuffed animals and crayons and books and pictures but the children themselves the mothers of their own children now so that it is as if the children they themselves used to be simply ceased to exist along with the young man I once was. There is no telling the sweet sadness of all that—of the Woodland Road house gone as completely as a dream when you wake up and as haunting as a dream, and the Vermont house still there but home no longer.

Where do you look for the home you long for if not to the irrecoverable past? How do you deal with that homesickness of the spirit which Antonio Parr speaks of, that longing for whatever the missing thing is that keeps even the home of the present from being true home? I only wish I knew. All I know is that, like Antonio, I also sense that something of great importance is missing which I cannot easily name and which perhaps can never be named by any of us until we find it if indeed it is ever to be found. In the meanwhile, like Gideon and Barak and the others, I also know the sense of sadness and lostness that comes with feeling that you are a stranger and exile on the earth and that you would travel to the ends of that earth and beyond if you thought you could ever find the homeland that up till now you have only glimpsed from afar. Where do you go to search for it? Where have I myself searched?

I have come to believe that for me the writing of books may have been such a search although it is only recently that I have thought of it that way. For forty years and more I have been at it, sitting alone in a room with a felt-tip pen in my hand and a notebook of unlined white paper on my lap for anywhere from three to five hours a day on the days when I work. Whether it is a novel I'm writing or a work of nonfiction, at the start of each day I usually have some rough idea of where I plan to go next, but at least as often as not that is not where I end up going, or at least not in the way I foresee or at the pace I intend. Time slows down to the point where whole hours can go by almost without my noticing their passage and often without writing anything at all. Sounds tend to fade away—somebody running a power mower, a dog barking in the driveway, voices speaking in another part of the house. Things that have been bothering me disappear entirely—the television set that needs to be repaired, the daughter we haven't heard from for over a week so that I am certain some terrible disaster has befallen her, my wretched defeat in a political argument at a dinner party the evening before.

In between periods of actually writing down words on the white page before me, my eyes almost always glance off to the left toward the floor, but it is not the floor that I am seeing. I am not really seeing anything or doing anything in the usual sense of the term. I am simply *being*, but being in what is for me an unusually intense and unfocused manner. I am not searching for the right way to phrase something, or for the next words to have a character speak, or for how to make a graceful transition from one paragraph to another. As nearly as I understand the process, I am simply letting an empty place open up inside myself and waiting for something to fill it. And every once and so often, praise God, something does. The sign that reads WELCOME HONE. The character who speaks something closer to the truth than I can imagine having ever come to on my own. A sentence or two in a sermon, perhaps, that touch me as usually only something I haven't seen coming can touch me or that feed me as if from another's hand with something that I hadn't realized I was half starving for. I think it is not fanciful to say that among the places I have searched for home without realizing what I was doing is that empty and fathomless place within myself and that sometimes, from afar, I may even have caught a glimpse of it in the shadows there.

Sometimes, I suspect, the search for home is related also to the longing of the flesh, to the way in which, both when you are young and for long afterward, the sight of beauty can set you longing with a keenness and poignance and passion, with a kind of breathless awe even, which suggest that beneath the longing to possess and be possessed by the beauty of another sexually—to *know* in the biblical idiom—there lies the longing to know and be known by another fully and humanly, and that beneath that there lies a longing, closer to the heart of the matter still, which is the longing to be at long last where you fully belong. "If ever any beauty I did see, / Which I desir'd, and got, 'twas but a dream of thee," John Donne wrote to his mistress ("The Good Morrow"), and when I think of all the beautiful ones whom I have seen for maybe no more than a passing moment and have helplessly, overwhelmingly desired, I wonder if at the innermost heart of my desiring there wasn't, of all things, homesickness.

Finally, as I ask myself where I have searched, I think of another winter—not the winter of 1934 in East Liberty but the winter of 1953 in New York City, when I was a twenty-seven-year-old bachelor trying to write a novel which for one reason or another refused to come to life for me, partly, I suspect, because I was trying too hard and hadn't learned yet the importance of letting the empty place inside me open up. Next door to where I lived there happened to be a church whose senior minister was a man named George Buttrick, and depressed as I was about the novel and with time heavy on my hands, I started going to hear him preach on Sunday mornings because, although I was by no means a regular church-goer, somebody told me he was well worth hearing, as indeed he proved to be. What I discovered first was that he was a true believer, which in my experience a great many preachers are not. Maybe in some intellectual, theological way they believe everything I do, but there is no passion in their belief that either comes through to me or seems to animate them. Buttrick couldn't have been less of a pulpit-pounder, but his passion was in his oddly ragged eloquence and in the way he could take words you had heard all your life and make you hear them and the holiness in them as though for the first time. These were also the days before ministers were supposed to be everybody's great pal and to be called by their first names from the word go, the trouble with which, at least for me, is that it's not another great pal that I go to church looking for, but a prophet and priest and pastor. Buttrick for me became, wonderfully, all three, and although I have never met a warmer, kinder man, we never became pals, for which I am grateful, and if there was anybody in his congregation who called him George, I never happened to hear it.

It was toward the middle of December, I think, that he said something in a sermon that has always stayed with me. He said that on the previous Sunday, as he was leaving the church to go home, he happened to overhear somebody out on the steps asking somebody else, "Are you going home for Christmas?" and I can almost see Buttrick with his glasses glittering in the lectern light as he peered out at all those people listening to him in that large, dim sanctuary and asked it again—"Are you going home for Christmas?"—and asked it in some sort of way that brought tears to my eyes and made it almost unnecessary for him to move on to his answer to the question, which was that home, finally, is the manger in Bethlehem, the place where at midnight even the oxen kneel.

Home is where Christ is was what Buttrick said that winter morning and when the next autumn I found myself to my great surprise putting aside whatever career I thought I might have as a writer and going to Union Seminary instead at least partly because of the tears that kept coming to my eyes, I don't believe that I consciously thought that home was what I was going there in search of, but I believe that was the truth of it.

Where did my homeward search take me? It took me to the Union Seminary classrooms of four or five remarkable teachers as different from each other as James Muilenburg of the Old Testament department, who was so aflame with his subject that you couldn't listen to him without catching fire yourself, and John Knox of the New Testament department, who led us through the Gospels and Paul with the thoroughness and delicacy of a great surgeon, yet who were alike in having a faith which continues to this day to nourish mine although it has been almost forty years since the last time I heard their voices. When I was ordained in Dr. Buttrick's church in 1958, the search set me on a path that has taken me to places both in the world and in myself that I can't imagine having discovered any other way.

It took me to Phillips Exeter Academy in the 1960s, where I tried to teach and preach the Christian faith to teenage boys, a great many of whom were so hostile to the idea of religion in general and at the same time so bright and articulate and quick on their feet that for nine galvanizing, unnerving years I usually felt slow-witted and tongue-tied and hopelessly square by comparison. It took me and continues to take me every now and then to people in the thick of one kind of trouble or another who, because they know of my ordination, seek me out for whatever they think I may have in the way of comfort or healing, and I, who in the old days would have shrunk with fear from any such charged encounter, try to find something wise and hopeful to say to them, only little by little coming to understand that the most precious thing I have to give them is not whatever words I find to say but simply whatever, spoken or unspoken, I have in me of Christ, which is also the most precious thing they have to give me. All too rarely, I regret to say, my search has taken me also to a sacred and profoundly silent place inside myself, where it is less that I pray than that, to paraphrase Saint Paul, the Holy Spirit itself, I believe, prays within me and for me "with sighs too deep for words" (Romans 8:26).

In recent years the homeward search has taken me as a writer to distant worlds which I never before would have guessed were within the range of my imagination. In eleventh-century England I have heard an old hermit named Godric, aghast at how he has come to be venerated, say, "To touch me and to feel my touch they come. To take at my hands whatever of Christ or comfort such hands have. Of their own, my hands have nothing more than any man's and less now at this tottering, lame-wit age of mine when most of what I ever had is more than mostly spent. But it's as if my hands are gloves, and in them other hands than mine, and those the ones that folk appear with roods of straw to seek. It's holiness they hunger for, and if by some mad chance it's mine to give, if I've a holy hand inside my hand to touch them with, I'll touch them day and night. Sweet Christ what other use are idle hermits for?" (*Godric* [San Francisco: Harper & Row, 1983], p. 43).

I have stood by the fifth-century Irish saint Brendan the Navigator as he preached to some ragged bog people he had just converted and have heard him "tell them news of Christ like it was no older than a day. . . . He'd make them laugh at how Christ gulled the elders out of stoning to death a woman caught in the act of darkness. He'd drop their jaws telling them how he hailed Lazarus out of his green grave and walked on water without making holes. He'd bring a mist to their eyes spinning out the holy words Christ said on the hill. . . and how the Holy Ghost was a gold-eyed milk-white dove would help them stay sweet as milk and true as gold" (*Brendan* [San Francisco: Harper & Row, 1988], pp. 49, 48).

And I have traveled back to that day, somewhere in the second millennium B.C. perhaps, when Jacob stole Esau's blessing from their blind old father, Isaac, and heard him say, "It was not I who ran off with my father's blessing. It was my father's blessing that [like a runaway camel] ran off with me. Often since then I have cried mercy with the sand in my teeth. I have cried *ikh-kh-kh* to make it fall to its knees to let me dismount at last. Its hind parts are crusted with urine as it races forward. Its long-legged, hump-swaying gait is clumsy and scattered like rags in the wind. I bury my face in its musky pelt. The blessing will take me where it will take me. It is beautiful and it is appalling. It races through the barren hills to an end of its own" (*The Son of Laughter* [San Francisco: HarperCollins, 1993], pp. 85–86).

Those are some of the places the search has taken me, and what can I honestly say I have found along the way? I think the most I can claim is something like this. I receive maybe three or four hundred letters a year from strangers who tell me that the books I have spent the better part of my life writing have one way or another saved their lives, in some cases literally. I am deeply embarrassed by such letters. I think, if they only knew that I am a person more often than not just as lost in the woods as they are, just as full of darkness, in just as desperate need. I think, if I only knew how to save my own life. They write to me as if I am a saint, and I wonder how I can make clear to them how wrong they are.

But what I am beginning to discover is that, in spite of all that, there is a sense in which they are also right. In my books, and sometimes even in real life, I have it in me at my best to be a saint to other people, and by saint I mean life-giver, someone who is able to bear to others something of the Holy Spirit, whom the creeds describe as the Lord and Giver of Life. Sometimes, by the grace of God, I have it in me to be Christ to other people. And so, of course, have we all—the life-giving, life-saving, and healing power to be saints, to be Christs, maybe at rare moments even to ourselves.

I believe that it is when that power is alive in me and through me that I come closest to being truly home, come closest to finding or being found by that holiness that I may have glimpsed in the charity and justice and order and peace of other homes I have known, but that in its fullness was always missing. I cannot claim that I have found the home I long for every day of my life, not by a long shot, but I believe that in my heart I have found, and have maybe always known, the way that leads to it. I believe that Buttrick was right and that the home we long for and belong to is finally where Christ is. I believe that home is Christ's kingdom, which exists both within us and among us as we wend our prodigal ways through the world in search of it.

2

❖ ❖ ❖ ❖ ❖

The Schroeders Revisited

Introduction

These poems are about the Schroeder family, who appeared first in a novella of mine called *The Wizard's Tide*, which was written for children but considered too grown up for them and thus published for grown-ups or grown-up children instead. A few explanatory notes are in order.

At center stage is Teddy Schroeder, his younger brother, Billy, and their parents, Ted and Connie, all of whom are represented by a poem apiece. The one about Connie is written as if by Teddy as is also the one about Teddy's father, Ted. There are poems too about Teddy's Schroeder grandparents, his two Schroeder uncles, Phil and Jeff, and their sister, his Aunt Millie. Another poem is about Teddy's great-grandfather Jacob August Ruprecht (his grandmother Schroeder's father and the family patriarch), who as a small boy in 1849 traveled in a covered wagon across the continent with his

German immigrant family to take part in the California Gold Rush. Another poem is about a pair of German sisters named Anna and Rosa, who worked for Teddy's grandparents for many years. Teddy called his maternal grandmother Dan, the person whom next to his mother he loved more than anyone else, and two poems are hers, followed by one about her only son, Teddy's Uncle Jimmy. The last poem of all is about Teddy as a senior citizen remembering his father, or trying to.

When Teddy was ten, his father committed suicide, and seven years later his father's youngest brother, Jeff, did the same thing. One way or another most of the poems reflect one or both of these seminal events. The one about Grandma Schroeder shows her in her New York apartment the day she returned from New Jersey, where her son Ted died while she was visiting there. She has just broken the news to her husband.

Careful readers of *The Wizard's Tide* will note various discrepancies. For example, in the book Teddy has a kid sister known as Bean, who in the poems has been transformed into a kid brother named Billy. In the book Teddy's father takes his life by one method and in the poems by another. And so on. My only explanation is that in the world of the imagination, just as in the world we imagine to be real, there are mysteries beyond explaining. In addition to that, it is perhaps necessary to add only that *The Wizard's Tide* is set in the depression years of the 1930s but that most of the poems remember those days from a considerably later period.

Ted Schroeder

On my father's last dawn
I remember he opened the door.
I remember he closed the door.
I remember no thing he said if he said
a thing. Goodbye, boys.
Teddy and Billy, goodbye.
I am going downstairs.
I am going to turn on the car.
I am going to sit on the running board
and hold my head in my hands.
The two terrible women I love
will look after you. Your mother
will be a good mother but beware
of her tongue. Your grandmother
will pay the bills but beware.
I have left your mother a note only she will find.
I have showered and shaved.
I have combed my hair in the mirror.
I have dressed in clean clothes.
Your mother is still asleep in her bed
or pretending to sleep. As I passed
my mother's door I could hear her dreaming.
I have opened your door at the top of the stairs.
Now I will close your door and go down
in my gray slacks and maroon sweater,
my fresh shirt, my hair damp from the shower,
my note on the last page

of the book your mother is reading,
and start up the Chevy and wait
till it gets me where I am going.
Boys, I can leave you only the world.
I can leave the world only you.
Go away from this house.

Grandma Schroeder

My husband won't come to the table.
You can take him a glass of milk to his room.
Just bring me a tray here by the window
where I hear the horns of the cars on Park coming home,
where I see the last of the sun from my chair.

You can say I have gone if the phone rings.
You can say we've both gone unless it's one of the boys.
Theirs were the second and third of our hearts to break.
Mine was the first. My husband's is only now.
He's lying on top of his bed with his Scotch.
He's not wearing his teeth. His eyes look splintered
like glasses. I don't know what he sees.
Maybe the Sheepshead Bay summers,
my father's big house on Millionaires' Row,
the three boys so handsome and strong then, all three.

It's as if I have spent my whole life at this window
waiting for Rosa to enter the room
and lay some unbearable message down on the table.
I have borne it. I have brought the news home
to my husband. I have not moved from this chair.

The clouds are like china laid out on a golden table.
Across 81st Street the sun flashes back from a window.
Already the dusk lies thick as dust in this room.
In my husband's place there is only his empty chair.
If I sit here the rest of my life, will I ever be home?

Grampa Schroeder

We were trolling for bluefish off Rockaway Point in August
of nineteen ought seven with four or five friends and some
    beer.
Tom Pulaski was running the Humming Bird's naphtha
    motor.
We'd had a fair catch. It was late afternoon and we'd started
for shore where Louise and the children were spending the
    week
in her father's big gingerbread house on the water when
    I heard
in the distance some voices calling for help and ordered
Pulaski to put on top speed. A launch had capsized
with a man and his wife clinging on to the bottom and one
other woman some ten yards away who was struggling for
    life
in a white dress and before we could reach her went down
for the last time in the combers in sight of us all.
We threw ropes to the two still afloat and hauled them
    aboard.
The story appeared in the *Brooklyn Eagle* with me
as the hero for saving their lives, which I did, and Louise
clipped it out and pasted it into the family scrapbook
crammed full of her father's doings: the night that Carl
    Schurz
made a speech from the porch of their Brooklyn house,
    his honors,
his brewery, his endless accounts of the Gold Rush trek
he made as a boy with his father in 'forty-nine

in a covered wagon, his mother and baby sister
dying en route and all that. If they gave me a nickel
for each time I've heard him tell it in clouds of smoke
from his Cuban cigar, his potbelly sprinkled with ash
and his whiskers stained yellow, I'd be a rich man. I have
    never
been rich. My business went down in the Crash. We have
    lived
on the money the old man left. I sit at the head
of the table but Louise pays the bills. She keeps me in Scotch
and smart clothes and tobacco, coughs up for the summers
    in Quogue,
the chauffeur, the college tuitions. I stroll in the Park
with my cane and my gimpy leg. I stop for a glass
or two with my friends coming home. I've lost all my teeth
in more ways than one. Louise has grown fat as her father
and more. She locks up the liquor. She says I'm no longer
the man she married, whoever he was—a young sport
in a boater who liked to go trolling for bluefish and one
afternoon saved two people from drowning and watched
    as the third
was lost in the combers never guessing the luck was all hers.

Uncle Jeff

The *Tribune* showed him in glasses
his hair slick from the shower
named to a key job
at age forty-one his face
full of zest for presents still
to be opened who could prove DeVere
wrote Shakespeare and quote from Houseman
forever a husband true
to his wife except for one other
lady he loved for whom maybe
his half-smile in the *Trib*
was intended his eyes cocky
and bright with his secret the rising
star in a family of falling
stars a father who failed
and a brother the oldest and sweetest
who fell by his own hand
on a fall morning the brother
whom he more than anyone else
blamed for leaving them all
in his dust then followed a few
years later maybe because
of the army turning him down
or something to do with the lady
God only knows but one spring
after buying the Sunday papers

and asking the maid about breakfast
he went upstairs forever
a rising star to rise
no higher a shooting star
almost too quiet to hear.

Uncle Phil

Slipping in at the shallow end backwards,
only his fuzzy shoulders, his bald head,
breaking the surface of sky,
he sculls to deep water intent
on not rippling the treetops' stillness,
his face afloat among clouds
in the pool of his rich friends
in the mountains, old comic caught
between acts till the gin begins
and he's tossing pancakes at supper,
bucking and winging his way away
from the missed chances, the two
missing brothers, the mother
he rings every morning, the wife.
Submerged to his lips,
He says, *I dream every night*
I'm alone in the city.
I've lost the address of Mother and Father.
I can't find my way.

Aunt Millie

I can't remember my children's childhood
the sweet things they said or saying sweet things
or getting them ready for school or the ribbons
they wore in their hair or brushing their hair

I forget the voices they had as children
the sound of them calling my name and even
the name they called me not mother some other
thing they made up some forgotten name

I would spike my juice in the morning then maybe
again before lunch like a bum in a blizzard
afraid if the fire goes out he will freeze
in the snow he will die till by supper my face

was a stranger's face and my voice the voice
of a prompter feeding me lines to a play
I despised and my husband and children part
of some other play that had no part for me

I remember the snows of my childhood walking
to school through the Park with my brothers Teddy
the one I called Ceddie he hated it so
and I loved him so much and Phil with the dimpled

chin the girls flocked to and Jeff fresh as paint
the brightest of all and oh I was proud
to be with them wearing my hair to the waist
with a fur toque and a muff of gray squirrel

in the snow past the frozen pond with the skaters
the carousel shuttered for winter the sleighs
drawn by horses and on to the steps of Saint Agatha
at West 91st which still I remember

the sound of their voices the clouds of their breath
as they shouted goodbye from the dark gates
of Trinity School next door remember
my dream of waking some morning a boy

like them or having a beau with a dimpled
chin or a son to watch over his brothers
and plain little sister like Teddy who married
the wrong girl at the wrong time

and went up in a cloud of exhaust from his Chevy
his beautiful face gone hollow-eyed haunted
not knowing that seven years later the way
we had followed his path through the white snow

in the Park past the empty zoo and the stone
angel Jeff with a single shot
before breakfast one morning would follow him once
again through the dark gates and I

have forgotten everything since or almost
forgotten and what I remember I never
tell to the strangers who live in this house
where only the fire saves me from freezing.

Great-grandfather Ruprecht

(1) To each child: a million in cash and a Steinway grand,
A share in the brewery and the Brooklyn land.

To Frida: my bitter tongue as well,
Horse sense, my subway map of Hell.

To Emma: her mother's lovely face and memory
Of how I caused her mother's misery.

To Tony: my strong views, weak eyes,
a monkey's intelligent, gold-rimmed gaze.

To Louise: my brawn and brass to bear the knocks
Of fate enough to fell an ox.

To Budelein: all the tears I never shed,
My belly laugh, sweet dreams in bed.

(2) Hermann and August, sons, to you I leave
my father's diary of the nine-month nightmare
trek he took us on in quest of California
gold in 'forty-nine, my brother Jacob
Frederick, age fifteen, myself, eleven,
our baby sister, two, and her whom even
mother seems not dear enough a name
to call her dearness by, leaving Brooklyn
seventy Germans strong on twenty March
with Father leading, first stop Philadelphia
(raining cats and dogs), next Pittsburgh (smoky)
by canal, and then the steamer "Enterprise"

to chug us on to where the glorious Ohio
meets the Mississippi, Father (Father
said) of Waters, finally Independence
where we pitched our tents and after four weeks' time
to gather horses, wagons, forty cows,
five yoke of oxen, started west.
One day I counted more than eighty broken
wagons left to rot and sixteen hundred
cattle dead for lack of grass and water.
Dysentery, diarrhea, scurvy, thirst
took their toll of Germans. Once we reached
the Rockies the five of us were on our own.
When our oxen died we drank their blood, had just
a two-wheeled cart to lug what little gear
we hadn't ditched. The Indians had faces painted
blue and red, their horses strung with beads.
The buffalo had crisp, black locks. A grocery-selling Dane
named Lassen charged us our last cent for scrapings
of potato soaked in vinegar for saving Father's
life. In the Sierras the baby died
of teething fever beneath a canvas stretched
on poles. Mother died near Bidwell's Bar
at Christmas, buried coffinless beside the river
Feather by Fred and me with Father still
too sick to dig. All the gold we ever
panned was barely gold enough to buy
our passage home by way of Panama.
My father's diary does not tell the tale
he told a doctor at our camp some weeks

before my mother's death who gave some salve
to ease her blackened eye and poor, cut cheek.
My father said she'd fallen from the cart.
"Love-licks?" the doctor said and winked at him.

(3) I lunch at Lüchow's Wednesdays with old friends.
On Fridays at the Kegel Klub I bowl
with men whose signatures adorn the silver
loving cup they gave me on my eightieth—
Pfizenmayer, Berthold, Wachter, Schock.
The New York Liederkrantz where I sang baritone
for years made me their president. My chauffeur
Higgins, once my coachman, holds my nightshirt
out so I can pull it over me in one
great swoop and at the same time step into
my slippers. Each moment saved is money saved.
My winter living room looks north on Central Park.
In summers all my children visit me
at Millionaires' Row in Sheepshead Bay
and all their children numbering twenty-two
plus four of the next generation down.
With my Van Dyke I look like Buffalo Bill
grown stout with bulging eyes. Sometimes at meals
my temper flares. A grandson spills his milk.
A son-in-law is slow to hold my chair.
Then suddenly my fist comes down with such a crash
That I myself am thunderstruck and see
The Sheepshead dining room as Bidwell's Bar.
My children drop their jaws and stare at me

with Mother's frightened eyes. I strike at them
like Father with my fist for fearing me.
I strike at Father for the fear I felt
of him all washed with reverence and love like gold
and gravel in a pan. But my worst blow
is for the eleven-year-old I was, too weak
and craven to protect the broken face
that haunts me even as I walk up Fifth
and hurl my cane ahead of me, then stoop
for it, to keep in trim; or play at skat;
or smoke cigars and watch the boats. Weakness
worse than scurvy is the curse of pioneers.

(4) Hermann, August, daughters, my strength
is my bequest to you. With it my rage.
Forgive in me the chicken-hearted child
I can't forgive, the father that I had
and am, the husband that I was.

Connie Schroeder

Maybe the worst she did was
say I was pimply, say
I was chinless and ugly, I

for whom she of them all
was most beautiful, needed
the most, or maybe the worst

was to make me (her child)
her father and bosom friend,
her husband, to say I was

beautiful, need me
the most. Maybe the worst I
did was across a green

lawn to wing a peach at
the worst of her, standing so
gold in the sun, so deadly, or

maybe the worst was to say
You first killed my
father, now you are killing

me, and she said what
I'd said made it easier now
to do what would have to be

done, never naming whatever
it was, the unnameable
thing. In time she took

to keeping her eyes tight
shut when she talked, she
heard almost nothing you

couldn't shout, she said her knees
bent the wrong way when she
walked, and three husbands

and ninety years old she said
what she was was the last rose
of summer, but to the end

when she struck, she struck
to kill, and the worst she
could think of she said,

the most terrible things she knew
how to say, and we laughed
till the tears came when I

told her I'd smelled her
smoking at night in the john
and she said she'd been smoking

at both ends, or the time she
said there was something so *cheap*
about babies, or once at the circus

when monkeys were riding
bikes with a third wheel
for balance she said with

deep scorn *There's nothing*
they won't do to give
those damned monkeys a break.

The last time I saw her she said
Why do you hate me? and I
remembered when I was in

fourth grade how she'd pick me
up after school. It was
spring, and the smell

of the car was the smell of
spring and of her and of going
home, and I loved her more

than I knew how to say, more
than I know how to say
to this day or will ever know.

Teddy

He hears the Jamaican cook groan
making supper she smells like lemons
she hasn't been paid for weeks
hears Uncle Don on his brother's
Donald Duck Philco his parents
downstairs having drinks
his mother's voice angry the empty
voice of his father like empty
rooms in the house where nothing
awful is happening but waiting
to happen he watches and waits
the slam of a door the car
not there in the morning
now that his father is dead
and his children not far from his father's
age when he died now
that he cannot remember his father's
face or even remember
how once he remembered
and the awful thing fifty years past
and nothing but good things happening
still even now he strains
to weave from the silence at night
the sound of a car coming home
hears only the beat of his heart
like the heart of a child.

Billy

We'd tinker with things in the yard,
oiling the mower, raking
the cut grass, coiling
the hose, or in the garage
sorting old nails or washing
the car. Daddy was mine.
Mommy was Teddy's. She took
him to see the *Mikado*, made him
a crown out of cardboard, rings
on his fingers. When Daddy was dead,
you wouldn't have known he had eaten
or slept in our house or been sad
there or happy, his name never named,
and once when they found me crying
under the bed they didn't
know why.

Rosa and Anna

On our afternoon off in the Park one Sunday we found
him under a green bench with his broken wing
fanned out in the dust and I knew we must bring
him home with us, Anna and I, so we wrapped around

him my blue wool scarf and Herr Schroeder made him
   a splint
from a wooden match and Frau Schroeder said when he
   was cured
we must take him back where he came from. She wanted
   no bird
and its droppings at 940 Park. And ever since

we have kept him hidden. He sits on the windowsill
in the sun in our cell of a room on the court where at times
a three-piece brass band plays for nickels and dimes
tossed down out of windows, or if I am sitting still

cleaning silver or if Anna is soaking her sore feet
or shelling peas he will flutter his way through the air
and land on our shoulders to pluck at strands of our hair
or tickle us under our chins with his hard little beak.

At night he sleeps on top of the dresser beside
the Holy Mother of God. One evening before
dinner, Herr Schroeder peered in through the dining room
   door
and saw him picking his way through the silver knives

and forks on the table, the best linen napkins, the glass
dish of celery and olives. *Verdammte Taube!* he said
with his pipe in his teeth, but thank God that instead
of storming out into the kitchen, he let it pass

and said nothing. We have worked for this family since time
    began.
We have seen the children grow up and leave. We have wept
over poor Mr. Ted. We have served them their meals and
    swept
their floors. We are both old maids not counting the man

in the band on the boat coming over who made me his wife
for just long enough to run off with my savings. We have
    known
good times along with the bad. We have walked on the dunes
at Quogue in the summers. We have eased a little the life

of our family in Germany sending them money. Each year
we've sailed back for a visit and been treated like queens
by nieces and nephews who think we are rich. We have seen
Philadelphia and Boston. We have made some friends here.

But when Hansi took bread crumbs out of our hands,
his neck a rainbow of colors, his feathered breast
soft as a baby's cheek, we forgot all the rest.
He was our hidden heart's treasure, our two lives' best
    chance.

Dan

I told Constance I never shed a tear
when Ted died. You don't shed tears in an earthquake.
You run for your life or stand in a doorway.
Five days later Ted's father died of a broken
heart so the letter I'd already started
to him and his wife I had to tear up
and replace with another only to her,
wondering how the poor dear could survive.
It must be the Germans' blood, that Stygian
stream, that bears them through even the horrors
they bring on themselves let alone on the world.

My father was French, from Geneva, and came here
to fight in the Civil War and help free
his black brothers. *Les Enfants Perdus* was his regiment's
name, and in front of Petersburg he was felled
by a sniper's bullet and died of the wound
some years later in terrible pain, to be buried,
alas, in a pauper's grave. He had lovely,
sad eyes and wrote in his copperplate hand
a tale just for me called *La Fée aux Roses*.
My mother was old New England and died
of consumption before I was one and so little
and dark in my white baby dress they told me
I looked like a spider drowned in a saucer
of milk and wasn't expected to live out
the year. I have lived out ninety, thus proving
not only the Germans survive.

                                        I think
of my life as a play I've enjoyed. The Tennessee
walker I rode as a girl. The visits
to France when the children were young. The flush
Pittsburgh years in the Woodland Road house with Williams
the cook, and the chauffeur named wondrously Gear,
and grim Ellen to bring me just at eleven
my buttermilk served on a silver tray.
When I found that my husband was having a fling
with a lady the scandal sheets billed as the Stolen
Princess, some said I should leave him. But why?
I knew it would pass, and it did, and for better
than thirty years more we were friends, and sometimes,
finding him lost in the evening papers,
I would lean from behind and kiss him on top
of his bald old head, and every so often
I miss him the way I miss the sound
of the foghorns in Maine, where we summered for years
by the sea, and the fog, and the creaking of gulls.

Teddy's the one of my grandsons I tell
of such things because he will listen for hours
to all my old tales and thinks the sun rises
and sets on me, sitting there round-eyed and asking
me always for more although now he's grown up
you'd think he'd have other things on his mind.
When his Uncle Jeff took his life like his brother
before him, I wrote Teddy he mustn't believe
he sails under some family curse, and I pray

that is true, or would pray if I only were sure
someone's listening. Who knows? For the lad's sake and also
for mine, I hope he'll sail into the twenty-first
century with a memory or two in his grips
of a wordy old citizen born two years after
the death of Abe Lincoln, how she lost a father
as he did, and almost a husband, and lived
to tell him again and again how it was.

Dan (2)

Years later, one breakfast burns still like sun
in the bowl of a spoon. Unitarians believe
in at most, you said, one God, and you called him
to witness: *My God!*—with skeins of smoke
from your Chesterfield, the marmalade in flames, the star
from your coffee aswing on the crazy ceiling—
How I hate these four people!
Your husband bald as his breakfast egg.
Mounting his muffin, the mad dauphin your son.
Your handsome, blue-eyed daughter. And I,
your pimply, rapt idolater.
A joke. We took it so.
Your eyes, buzzard-amber and burning,
neither hated nor loved but were bored, bored,
my dear dead dear—bored with Carolina sun,
with mountains rising like smoke, with your eighty-five
    years,
but boredom like a coif, a transcendence,
like Solomon in all his great and tiresome glory.

Uncle Jimmy

My tiddly uncle climbed a tree, sat hours
hairy and black in a forked branch with his smile
hung crooked, his oystery sneakers jutting like fungus.
Through the sleeping-porch screen we watched dampness
    fall
until there were pearls in his eyes,
and my grandfather pounded the trunk with his stick:
Come down, sir! Come down from that tree!
My uncle should never have called him an old gray rat
and swung him around till his glasses fell off on the carpet,
should never have climbed there at all, I thought,
assuming he'd have to come down in the end and make
    everything
right. But he never came down. Summers, summers,
have come and gone, and the old gray rat has been caught
in a fool-proof trap, and now where the sleeping porch was
there is nothing but sleep. Only my uncle hangs on.
Strangers no longer can tell him apart from the tree,
a hairy, black tree shelved all over with fungus,
with branches crooked as smiles, and at certain times,
in certain kinds of rain, as gray as pearls.

Ted Schroeder Remembered

The old tigers with prostates, the blue-haired vamps,
the barber who once lent him money, the child
he swam oceans ago on his shoulders—always
I sought the ones out who remembered my father
the swimmer, the dancer, the charmer of birds
from the trees; sought him under the pictures
in frames, at the bottoms of drawers, a boy
stretched out on the dunes in a jersey frowning,
or holding the ball with his year on his chest,
his stickpin, a letter that started out *Blessed*.
He went up in a puff of smoke in his thirties
leaving me in my sixties my father's Dutch uncle
to chide him for leaving so soon—before breakfast,
before we were up. In his roadster he waited
until the exhaust had exhausted him utterly
and not even the uncombed ladies in bathrobes
could get him back up on his feet.
What I pieced back together never did quite
do him justice, so I gave up the ghost,
and content myself now with occasional visits
to where he lies many years deep in my overgrown face.

Teddy to his Grandchildren

Until I finished them, I didn't see
that all these poems are yours. At best
I thought they were a way for me
once and for all to lay to rest

this family, all but one of whom I've lost,
with maybe a truth or two of who
they were, like farewell flowers tossed
into a grave. I never knew

that all the while within my heart,
unknowingly, I was in search of any
way I could to bring some part
of them to life so you, their children many

times removed, might have a sense
of how alive they were when I
first knew them as a child and hence
might even, as the years go by,

a little come to love them too.
If you could meet them, would they say,
as I suspect, that even though it's true
they knew much sadness in their day,

they're glad they lived at any cost?
That now at last they start to see
they've found more even than they lost?
Let it be so. Remember them for me.

3

◇　◇　◇　◇　◇

Letter to Benjamin

Dear Benjamin,

When you were born this summer in Burlington, Vermont,
your father decided to ask a few of us, rather than to give you
something on the order of a silver rattle or teething ring, to write
you a letter that you are to open on your twenty-first birthday,
August 25, 2015, which happens to fall on a Tuesday. It sounded
like a good idea when he suggested it, and it sounds like a good
idea still, but you can't imagine how I've struggled over it. I am
your grandfather, after all. I should have some extra special things
to say, and so I like to think I have, but the problem is how to de-
cide which ones to put in and which ones to leave out, where to
start and where to stop. My vision of your birthday itself keeps
getting in the way.

As I see it, your parents have taken a private room in a good
restaurant somewhere. Everybody is wearing evening clothes.
Dinner has been eaten. Toasts have been proposed over dessert

and coffee. The historic letters have been brought out in a cardboard box. You decide it might be entertaining to read a few of them out loud. You happen to pick out mine. What words of wisdom will it contain? What grandfatherly advice about the future? What revelations about the ancestral past? The prospect paralyzes me. If I am lucky enough to be there in the flesh, age eighty-nine, I will twitch with apprehension as you open the envelope. If I am there as a ghost, I will be tempted to drift out of the open window like a wisp of cigar smoke. How much less painful to give you a silver rattle. But a promise is a promise. I will do the best I can. I will forget about trying to be wise and grandfatherly. I will simply tell you a few of the things that seem important to me as I start writing this on the morning of Saturday, the 21st of October, 1994.

So I will start out once again with *Dear Benjamin* because it contains two important truths. The first is that you are indeed Benjamin, and the second is that to me you are indeed dear even though I hardly know you yet because at this point, when you are barely two months old, there really isn't much of you to know. You are dear because a little of my blood is in your veins, and therefore, as the old song goes, even when my song is over and done with, some echo at least of the melody will linger on in you. And you are dear because so many of the people I have loved in my life are somehow or other present in the genetic bouillabaisse of who you are even though you will know about many of them, if you know about them at all, only as names or old photographs in an album. Dear Benjamin.

When I look at those photographs myself—the earliest go back as far as my great-great- (your great-great-great-great-!) grandparents, who were born in the opening years of the nineteenth century some two hundred years ago as I write—I wonder who on earth they were. I've picked up a scrap or two about a few of them. My great-great-grandfather Isaac Golay on my mother's side, for instance. The picture I have shows him sitting in a chair with his left arm resting awkwardly on a table covered with a patterned shawl. He is wearing a frock coat that looks at least two sizes too big for him and has sleeves that come down over his knuckles. He is bald on top and seems to have brushed some of the side hair over his forehead a little to make him appear less so. He has impressive pouches under his eyes and is gazing out not quite directly at the camera with his brow slightly contracted and his lips drawn tight as though the photographer has just told him that if he so much as breathes for the next five minutes, the exposure will be completely ruined. He was a French Swiss who ran a jewelry business on the ground floor of his house in Geneva assisted by his wife, whose picture in a voluminous dress with a little bonnet tied under her chin is next to his in the album.

Her name was Rose Besançon Golay, she was of Huguenot descent, and the story is that she was more highly born than her husband and never let him forget it. Her photograph lends support to the theory. It shows her with clenched jaws looking at the camera out of the corner of her eyes with an expression of darkest suspicion. In response, perhaps, to the photographer's suggestion, she is trying to crank up a smile but has succeeded only in looking as mad as a wet French hen of Huguenot descent. Her chair is much grander than her husband's, as befits her station, and her left arm, like his, is resting on a table, except that on this one there are also two books, a very large one with another, much smaller, on top of it. You get the impression that if the photographer had been bold enough with that terrible glance upon him to suggest that she give her smile another try, she would have winged them both at him and in all likelihood would have scored a couple of bull's-eyes. But who knows what she and old Isaac were really like and what was going on inside them at the moment when the shutter snapped? All I can tell you is what little I picked up as the one member of my generation who was ever especially interested in such matters. And if this were a book instead of a birthday letter, who knows how long I would rattle on about them.

I would tell you, I'm sure, about my two grandmothers— about Naya, who spoke in shimmering paragraphs and was the one safe haven of my storm-tossed childhood, and about Grandma Buechner, who called a spade a spade and survived a series of family tragedies with a strength that I'm sure helped me survive them too although at the time I barely suspected it. I might tell you too about my great-great-grandfather Achazius Stehlin on my father's side, born in 1808, who gave up the idea of entering the priesthood for the law and became vice president of the short-lived Republic of Baden after the revolution of 1848, which, when it failed, led to his being condemned to death and sent to prison which he managed to escape for France and subsequently Brooklyn, New York, where upstairs in the saloon he ran (which his granddaughter, who was my grandmother, carefully explained was not a saloon in the vulgar sense but more of a *club*) he started what may have been the first German theater in America. And I would probably say a word or two about my great-grandmother Elizabeth Eimbke Buechner, who, when her dying husband complained about the noise she was making in his room with the carpet sweeper, is reported to have made a reply that has been enshrined in family legend. *"Heute ist Dienstag"* is what she said, which means "Today is Tuesday," because Tuesday was her day for sweeping the carpet no matter what.

Today happens to be Tuesday too. The sun is bright, and the sky is blue. Most of the autumn leaves have fallen, and the ones that are left on the trees are mostly rust-colored with here and there a feathering of lemon yellow. It is on the cool side, but our two dachshunds—Otto the Irrepressible and his uncle, Klaus the Long-suffering—seem perfectly comfortable dozing in the sun where the leaves lie thick and unraked. Last week as I drove along the unpaved West Pawlet road with the sun shining through them, they were as nearly golden as anything can be without being gold. They glistened and dazzled like the walls and vaulted ceiling of some great Arc de Triomphe so that I had no choice but to stop thinking about whatever I was thinking about and to think about them instead, less to think about them than just to lose myself in them. Did Achazius Stehlin, hot-footing it out of France one jump ahead of the posse, ever see leaves like that? Did Rose Besançon Golay ever catch a glimpse of them through the jewelry shop's grilled window, or did great-grandfather August Buechner at least hear them rustling maybe in between sweeps of the carpet sweeper? I like to believe so, but how can I ever know? I am appalled by how little I know even about my own grandfathers.

My grandfather Buechner died when I was ten, only a few days after the death of his oldest son, my father. He was a dapper old gentleman who loved fine clothes, fine food, good wine, and when his children were little loved taking them on walks through Central Park and showing them around museums. When his silk-importing business went under in 1929, he was more or less wiped out, and for the rest of his life the family had to live on his wife's inheritance, which wasn't easy for him and probably explains why in almost every memory I have of him he is holding a drink in his hand and not saying much. He and my grandmother lived for years in an apartment at 940 Park Avenue in New York, and once when I was spending the night there as a little boy, I found myself sleeping in a bed that for some reason had been made up without sheets, an event so unprecedented and confusing that, not knowing what else to do, I started to cry. My grandfather must have heard me as he passed by in the hall because all of a sudden there he was at my bedside in the dark asking me what the trouble was, and when I told him about the sheets, he said that once when he was about my age he had had to spend a night in a tree, where of course he had no sheets either. Since he had survived that experience no worse for wear, he said, he was sure that I would survive too. It gave me something else to think about anyway, and as far as I can remember that brief exchange was the nearest thing to a close encounter the two of us ever had. But if only I had gone further with it. If only I had asked him to tell me *why* he had spent the night in a tree. If only I had asked him to tell me more about himself. But I'm sure such questions never so much as crossed my mind at that age, and even if they had, I would never have dared ask them.

I was twenty-one years old, your age, when my grandfather Kuhn died—he was eighty-one—but although I saw a lot of him over the years, I never got to know him very well either. He was a shy, private sort of man, bald as an egg with liver spots on his shiny scalp, and a scruffy gray mustache, and a little pink papilloma round as a jellybean over one eyebrow. He not only loved my grandmother,

Naya, but enormously admired her wit and eloquence and always let her do most of the talking. I remember him sitting in the living room listening to the news of World War II on the radio with his straw hat on. He used to tell how when he was a young man he had eaten some black raspberries once in Somerset, Kentucky. He said they had made him so sick that he had never eaten black raspberries again, and for the rest of his life if he ever saw anybody else eating anything that struck him as questionable, he had only to intone Somerset, Kentucky, a couple of times in a baleful voice, and everybody knew exactly what he meant. I remember he hated to see my mother and her sister, Ruth, wearing jewelry for some reason, and when they were in a certain mood, they would tease him about it and to show their power over him would make him kiss their earrings. When my mother eloped with my father in 1922, he was so furious that he refused to see her for three or four years and had all the pictures of her put away and wouldn't allow anyone to mention her in his presence. He eventually relented, of course, and he and my father became friends although I can't remember ever seeing the two of them together or hearing him speak my father's name. Except once.

I must have been about fifteen or so and we were sitting on a screened porch in Tryon, North Carolina, when out of the blue he addressed me not as Buzzfuzz, which was what he had always called me before for some long forgotten reason, and not as Freddy, which was what just about everybody else called me, but as Fred, which was not so much my name as it had been my father's. The moment lasted no time at all, but I remember feeling that by using that name he was coming as close as he ever did to telling me that he was sorry—sorry that my father had died so young and sorry also for me. If only I had been able to press him further, but of course I wasn't and didn't, and since no such moment ever occurred between us again, he remained almost as shadowy a figure as my grandfather Buechner was.

But even if things had turned out otherwise, I wonder if it would have made any great difference. Even if my grandfathers had been less shadowy and I had been less timid, I wonder if I would ever have been able to learn from them what I would give so much to know now about who they were, both for its own sake and also for the sake of learning something more about who I am myself. Even if I were to stretch this letter out, God forbid, to a thousand pages, would I ever be able to convey my full story to you? I suspect the answer is no. I suspect that our stories in their fullness will always be hidden from each other and that all those whiskered old men and bonneted old women looking out at us from their photographs in the family album will always remain mysteries to us even if, like me, they happen to have written their memoirs. And yet I believe that all is not lost. Maybe we can never know each other's stories in their fullness, but I believe we can know them in their depth for the reason that in their depth we all have the same story.

Whether we're rich or poor, male or female, a nineteenth-century Swiss jeweler like Isaac Golay in his oversized frock coat, or a twentieth-century American clergyman like me with a penchant for writing books, or a young squirt celebrating his twenty-first birthday in the twenty-first century like you, our stories are all stories of *searching*. We search for a good self to be and for good work to do. We search to become human in a world that tempts us always to be less than human or looks to us to be more. We search to love and to be loved. And in a world where it is often hard to believe in much of anything, we search to believe in something holy and beautiful and life-transcending that will give meaning and purpose to the lives we live.

I sense a growing restlessness among the birthday guests. One of them keeps rolling up and unrolling a napkin. Another is glancing around the table wondering if it would be seemly to ask the waiter for an after-dinner drink. So enough of all this. Let's have another drink all around, this time on me, and as I raise my glass— whether I'm there in the flesh to do it or only as a benevolent ghost—my birthday wish is that after wandering through many a street for many a long year to come, you may find your way at last to the fountain in the square.

With love from your grandfather.

4

❖　❖　❖　❖　❖

Rinkitink in Oz

I still have the copy of *Rinkitink in Oz* that I read as a child—an early edition in putty-colored cloth with twelve color plates and a pictorial paper label on the front cover. It has stood up pretty well over the years, all in all. I must have been seven or eight when I penciled in my signature on the ownership page—THIS BOOK BELONGS TO: Freddy Buecher—leaving out the *n* in my last name for some reason. On the same page, also in pencil, I wrote down the letters and dial numbers of several radio stations: WOR 61, WJZ 55, WEAF 70, WABC 5 (I think I was wrong about WABC, which it seems to me should have been in the 80s somewhere). I was sick in bed a lot with a series of respiratory complaints as a child, and when I wasn't reading Oz books, I whiled away the time listening to programs like *Our Gal Sunday, Lorenzo Jones, Lum and Abner,* and the like. The pictorial label shows King Rinkitink and Prince Inga of Pingaree riding on the back of the cantankerous goat Bilbil—the background is a sunset orange at the bottom shading to pinkish yellow at the top, with Rinkitink holding Bilbil's horns like motorcycle handlebars—and just over Inga's left hip there is a scar on the label whose origins I can still account for.

I had left the book out in the sun at my grandparents' house on Woodland Road with a pink peppermint resting on top of it, and when I got back to it later, the peppermint had melted. I picked off what I could with my fingernail, taking some of the paper with it—hence the scar—and a little lower down, around Bilbil's shaggy hind legs, there are still traces of the peppermint itself hardened to a rough crust by the passage of half a century. I also colored in some of the black and white illustrations with wax crayons that must have been jumbo-sized because I had a hard time staying inside the lines with them, and Inga's purple tights bleed into his pointy-toed shoes, and Rinkitink's undersized golden crown stains the surrounding air yellow like sunshine. To reread the books of your childhood is to reread a page or two of your childhood itself. The Great Depression was on. My parents were living beyond their means, and we moved around a lot as my father kept changing jobs, to my mother's strident dismay. All was not well with my family, and even as a small boy I knew it. Among the happiest times I can remember from those years were the ones I lived in the Land of Oz.

Right from the beginning *Rinkitink* was my favorite Oz book and the one that from that day to this I have remembered in the greatest detail. To be sure, I loved all of the other ones too, but in many cases I have a hard time recapturing what went on in each. In which book does the Scarecrow find out that he is supposed to be the reincarnated Emperor Chang Wang Woe of the Silver Islands, for instance? In which do you find the monster Quiberon, who held the Ozure Isles in thrall, and in which of Ruggedo's many attempts to capture the Emerald City is he foiled by drinking the Water of Oblivion? But in the case of *Rinkitink*, I was never in any such doubt. At any point since first reading it I could have told you at the drop of a hat what Inga was doing when the fierce warriors of Regos and Coregos invaded his father's peaceful kingdom and by what mischance first the Pink Pearl and then the Blue Pearl were lost with consequences that nearly proved fatal. I could have described Bilbil's unrelenting irascibility and documented the sadistic cruelty of Queen Cor or explained how it happened that Zella, the charcoal burner's daughter, escaped being brutally stung when the swarm of bees attacked her for stealing their honey.

I identified most with Prince Inga, I think. He seemed about my age and, like me, was "somewhat too grave and thoughtful" as Baum describes him, loving nothing better than to climb up into his tree to read his sheepskins as I loved to hole up somewhere and read about Oz. "Now, if I am wise, and cautious, and brave, I believe I shall be able to rescue my father and mother," he whispers to himself at some point—it is his attempt to find the captured King and Queen of Pingaree that the plot of the book is all about—and although I'm sure that the connection never consciously occurred to me at the time, maybe at some dim level I sensed that Inga and I had that in common too. My father and mother needed rescuing no less than his. But most of all what I have remembered all these years is the great Rinkitink himself—Rinkitink the ebullient and irrepressible, bon vivant and singer of absurd songs, strong in his weakness and stout of heart in the face of despair. Without question, he is one of Baum's most brilliant creations, and I suspect that Baum himself knew it. "The Rinkitink story is considered by my family critics the jolliest and most interesting of my books," he wrote his publisher, Reilly, in 1915 when most of his books were behind him, and as far as I am concerned the family critics were dead right.

Apparently he wrote it around 1905 as a non-Oz book under the title *King Rinkitink* and then salted it away until 1915 when he fitted it out with a chapter of festivities in the Emerald City and other elements to establish it as one of the Oz series. By the time it was finally published in 1916, Baum was in the last two or three years of his life and seems to have known it. "If I am permitted to write another Oz book . . ." he wrote in his introduction to *Rinkitink*. He was suffering from severe attacks of angina complicated by an extremely painful facial tic douloureux together with gall bladder attacks and, according to his biographer, was dosing himself heavily with all the patent medicines and cure-alls he could lay his hands on. But 1905, when he wrote the original book, was in the middle of his golden and most productive years. *The Marvelous Land of Oz* came out in 1904 followed by *Queen Zixi of Ix* in 1905 and *John Dough and the Cherub* the next year. In 1906 too he began the Aunt Jane's Nieces series under the pseudonym of Edith Van Dyne. He was at the height of his powers, in other words, and starting with *The Marvelous Land of Oz* found himself a marvelous new illustrator in John R. Neill, who, in his illustrations for *Rinkitink,* anticipated the famous theatrical caricaturist Albert Hirschfeld by incorporating the names of friends or relations into some of his pictures. In Chapter Eight, for instance, there is a full-page rendering of Rinkitink and Inga seated at a table that bears among other delicacies a large bowl of fruit including several peaches, one of which has a fringe of fuzz on it spelling out in tiny letters *Virginia* in honor of his niece Virginia Long; and in Chapter Twenty-four one of the flowers that Rinkitink is soaring over on his swing has the face of a child and the name *Sonney* for his nephew John Upton, Jr., who at last report was alive and well and dividing his time between Vermont and Arizona. As for the source of the name Rinkitink, Baum may have found it in some doggerel by Laura E. Richards that includes the lines "In the Land of Rinkitink / All the happy people-weople / Never stop to think. . . . Happy Land of Rinkitink / I will go there too, I think." If that is indeed the case, it only goes to prove once again that even the most unpromising acorns can produce great oaks.

But back to the book itself and particularly to the character of Rinkitink. Surely nobody in the entire Oz canon ever made a more glorious entrance. He appears first in the second chapter being rowed to shore by twenty oarsmen in a big boat covered with a canopy of purple silk embroidered with gold. Rinkitink—so fat, Baum tells us, that he is nearly as broad as he is high—sits in a cushioned chair of state dressed to the nines in a purple silk robe that falls in folds to his feet and on his head a cap of white velvet with a circle of diamonds sewn around the band. Rising to his feet to wave to the stately royal family of Pingaree who have gathered on the shore to see who on earth is approaching, he is nearly toppled into the sea as the prow of his boat hits the beach, but nothing disconcerts him. "Well, here I am at last!" is his unforgettable opening line—nobody, of course, has the faintest idea who he is—and then for the first time we hear the peals of his unforgettable laughter. "Heh-heh-ho, ho, ho!" it begins, rising then into "Keek-eek-eek-eek!" and finally "Hoo, hoo, hoo, hoo!" In Neill's illustration of the moment, we see him with his head thrown back and his arms spread wide as the extraordinary sounds issue from him. One slippered foot is kicked forward, and his tunic strains over the swell of his enormous paunch. "Hush up!" says Bilbil the goat. "You're making yourself ridiculous." No wonder I have remembered it all these years.

Throughout the book, Bilbil plays the Fool to Rinkitink's Lear, sardonically reminding him every step of the way that he is making an idiot of himself, but whereas it takes Lear the better part of five acts to realize that such is indeed the case, Rinkitink from the beginning knows it as well as Bilbil does and rejoices in it. "Everything shall be done to make you comfortable and happy," says courtly, grave King Kitticut, to which Rinkitink, bursting into yet another peal of uproarious laughter, replies, "Why, that's my trouble. I'm too happy." It is the secret of his strength, needless to say. No danger or defeat can keep him down for long, and if idiocy is one thing to call it, the peace that passeth all understanding is another. Come hell or high water, his *joie de vivre* survives everything, and even when the wicked Queen Cor, threatening to use him as a human pincushion, forces him to sing one of his inane songs, although at the start of it he is racked with sobs, by the time he gets into high gear, he is belting it out as if he doesn't have a care in the world.

When Rinkitink ran away from his subjects because he decided that the duties of kingship were too confining, he took with him a parchment entitled *How to be Good*. It is full of profundities like "A Good Man is One who is never Bad" and "To avoid saying Unpleasant Things, always Speak Agreeably," and he finds it unendingly hilarious. But one of the elements that gives Baum's characterization such richness is the suggestion that the goodness of Rinkitink himself is something that can't be laughed at. Young Prince Inga is the one who puts it best. Bilbil, as usual, has been excoriating his master as an incompetent ninny, and Inga replies by saying, "But anyway his heart is kind and gentle and that is better than being wise," to which he then adds, "Let us forget everything but his good nature which puts new heart in us when we are sad." It put new heart in Inga anyway, and when I was Inga's age, it put new heart in me. Maybe that is the main reason why Rinkitink was always my favorite. Baum rarely if ever again created a hero so irresistible.

Nor, as far as I know, did he ever, either before or after, create villains as villainous as King Gos and Queen Cor of the twin islands. There are plenty of bad guys in the Oz books—one thinks of Ruggedo, the Nome King, of course, and Ugu the Shoemaker, Mombi, the Boolooroo of the Blues—but somehow theirs is a fairy-tale badness that never really chills the blood. Gos and Cor, on the other hand, are the real thing. They do not work their villainy with magic spells and outlandish transformations. They work it savagely and all too humanly with instruments that are no more magical than the ones that tyrants have used throughout history. Their enemies are condemned to hard labor in the mines, and when one of the women balks, Queen Cor threatens to flog her with a whip of seven lashes. When the King and Queen of Pingaree are handed over to the treacherous Kaliko for safekeeping, she urges him to treat them in a similar fashion. "They are rather delicate," she says, "and to make them work will make them suffer delightfully." She flies into a terrible rage at Inga when he inadvertently brushes her ear with a peacock fan and slaps him viciously twice with her big, hard hand. King Gos speaks of hanging people by the thumbs and throwing them into dungeons.

If Bilbil plays the Fool to Rinkitink's Lear, then Queen Cor is Goneril and Regan rolled into one and King Gos the bloodthirsty

Duke of Cornwall. Baum never wrote a book with more laughter and goodness in it than *Rinkitink*, but the evil that also stalks its pages is too humanly believable and close to home to shrug off as something that can be eliminated simply by a touch of Ozma's white magic. Kaliko can be made to behave by no more than the sight of a dozen eggs in Dorothy's basket, but the wickedness of Gos and Cor lies so deep in their hearts that the only way Baum found to extirpate it was by having them drowned on their voyage home from the Nome Kingdom. It is this believability of evil that gives the plot its urgency, and I can remember still the deep foreboding I felt as a child when Rinkitink and Inga lost the pink and blue pearls that protected them against all dangers and were left to the mercy of their merciless captors. Kaliko's pivoting rooms and murderous giants and flaming chasms—and Kaliko himself, for that matter—seemed mild and manageable by comparison. The darkness that Inga was to rescue his parents from was a true and chilling darkness, and as a small boy growing up in the midst of the Depression, I could sympathize with his plight.

Every fairy tale must have a happy ending, of course—a *eucatastrophe,* or sudden joyous "turn," as Tolkien calls it—and *Rinkitink* is no exception. Cor and Gos get their just deserts. The captive peoples are set free from their cruel bondage, and "with sobs and tears of joy," as Baum describes it, King Kitticut and Queen Garee are reunited with the son who has saved them. Only Bilbil is unmoved by the scene. "Joyful reunion, isn't it?" he comments. "But it makes me tired to see grown people cry like children." But then even Bilbil gets his turn. When the Wizard, resourceful and professional as always, hears him talk—only in Oz do animals have that gift, and Bilbil has never even been there—he realizes that the cynical old malcontent is really Prince Bobo of Boboland transformed into a goat by a wicked magician. It remains for Glinda the Good, through a complicated series of spells, to transform him in stages back into a handsome young man again, and in his proper form he begs Rinkitink to forgive him for having been so disagreeable over the years, explaining that his acid disposition was only part of the enchantment.

They all live happily ever after, in other words, or almost all. There is still Rinkitink to worry about. When all his adventures have come to a happy conclusion, one of his counselors turns up to take him back to his kingly duties in the capital city of Gilgad, and the fat little monarch puts up a terrible fuss. Neill's last color plate in the book shows him clinging to a post with a tragic expression on his face as the counselor, with a hand on his master's arm, tries bodily to drag him off to face his responsibilities. "What! Must I return to Gilgad and be forced to reign in splendid state when I much prefer to eat and sleep and sing in my own quiet way?" he wails. *Quiet* indeed. But his study of *How to be Good* pays off in the end, because he agrees that after three days of feasting he will finally to return to his people. The last we see of him is being rowed away in a boat where he is seated on a golden throne, and the last we hear from him is yet another song. "Is it a masterpiece, do you think?" he asks Prince Bobo, who responds in such a Bilbil-like way that one wonders if Glinda's transformation had been entirely successful. "Like all your songs, dear Rinkitink," he says, "the sentiment exceeds the poetry," with which words the book comes to an end.

As far as I know, Rinkitink appears in only one other Oz book, and that is *Lucky Bucky*. In the Emerald City there is a drive to keep the children from defacing public buildings with graffiti by having them instead decorate the castle walls with scenes of Oz history. Various Oz celebrities gather to help, and among them, we are told, is Rinkitink, "who had come a long way from his kingdom with a surly old goat to do their bit." Is it possible that in the end Prince Bobo decided that it had been more fun being Bilbil and persuaded Glinda to change him back to his previous incarnation? Or was it perhaps that during the time of his goathood he had begotten a son who grew up to inherit his father's disposition? As far as I know, the mystery remains unsolved to this day.

In order to Ozzify his non-Oz *King Rinkitink* manuscript of 1905, one of the ways Baum is supposed to have changed it in 1915 was to add the glittering feast that Ozma laid on in her gorgeous banqueting hall to celebrate the happy events with which the tale ends. Most of the great luminaries of Oz are in attendance. The Shaggy Man is there together with Jack Pumpkinhead, the Tin Woodman, and Cap'n Bill. Tiny Trot and Betsy Bobbin are there to keep Princess Dorothy company, and of course Ozma herself, who "outshone all her guests in loveliness," Baum says. The Hungry Tiger, the Cowardly Lion, the Glass Cat, and Hank the mule are on hand to represent the animal kingdom. Only the Scarecrow is missing— away on one of his periodic trips through the country, we are told— but he gets a chance to join in on the festivities later on.

It is undoubtedly true that Baum's chief reason for adding the scene was to make *Rinkitink* a proper addition to the Oz series, but I can't help wondering if, consciously or otherwise, he may have had another motive as well. With his health going from bad to worse and believing, as he wrote in his introduction, that this might be the last Oz book he would ever write, I can imagine the old romancer's simply wanting to bask one last time in the company of all his best friends. Rinkitink sings a song at the great gathering, and among the lyrics—written down by Dorothy on a piece of paper, Baum explains, and thus preserved for posterity—these verses occur:

> We're merry comrades all, to-night,
> Because we've won a gallant fight
> And conquered all our foes.
> We're not afraid of anything,
> So let us gayly laugh and sing
> Until we seek repose.
> So let's forget the horrid strife
> That fell upon our peaceful life
> And caused distress and pain;
> For very soon across the sea
> We'll all be sailing merrily
> To Pingaree again.

Although Baum lived to write several more Oz books before he laid down his pen for good, I cannot help believing that at the time he composed that valedictory song of hope and courage, he thought of it as just possibly his last farewell. And a song of hope and courage was exactly what the child I was needed most to hear.

5

◆　◆　◆　◆　◆

Of Whipples and Wheels

This is the dog
that worried the cat
that killed the rat
that ate the malt
that lay in the house that Jack built . . .

. . . so the old nursery rhyme goes, which is to say that to tell
the story of anything is to tell the story finally of everything. The
dog, the cat, the rat, the malt—you have to include all of them if
you are to do the story of Jack's house full justice, and you can't
stop with just them either. How about the man all tattered and
torn who kissed the maiden all forlorn, not to mention the priest
all shaven and shorn who was called in to officiate when they de-
cided to make things legal and settle down? Jack's house becomes
the hub of a wheel with endless spokes radiating out through time
and space in all directions, and the same is true of any house. Who
lived there first and where did they come from and who lived there

next, what did they do with their lives in that house and whose lives did their lives touch? The possibilities are endless.

It reminds you of the girl in Thornton Wilder's *Our Town* who received a letter addressed to the name of her town, her county, her state, her country, and then on to the Western Hemisphere, the Earth, the Solar System, the Universe, the Mind of God. If you do the thing right, not even the sky is the limit. So you settle for less, of course. You start at a point that appeals to you, mention only the spokes you know a little about and feel like mentioning, and stop where it seems like a good place to stop. In the case of the Old Whipple Mill in Shaftsbury, Vermont, you might do worse than start with an eccentric New Englander named Silas Hawes, who had a blacksmith shop in Shaftsbury in the early part of the last century. You might start eleven years before the War of 1812 had come to its inconclusive end.

The story goes that there was a tinware peddler who got this Hawes to shoe a horse for him one day, but, not having any ready cash, offered instead to pay him in kind. That was the way the peddler himself was apt to get paid, accepting dried apples or feathers or whiskey or old iron for his time, whatever his customers happened to have on hand. As luck would have it, one of the last payments he had received was in the form of some old saw blades, which may have been used for sawing marble or may have come from the kind of sawmill that had an up-and-down rather than a circular saw. In any event, the blades seemed to appeal to Hawes, and he accepted them. Whether he had already figured out what to do with them or whether it didn't occur to him until later, there is no way of knowing, but in either case they were to prove a turning point in his life, those blades. But first a word about the kind of man he was.

In 1872 Stephen A. Whipple wrote a letter in which he said, "Father says that Silas Hawes was the most singular man he ever knew," and since Stephen A. Whipple's father, Stephen Whipple the elder, was Hawes's partner, he had good reason to know. "Singular" was to put it mildly. Hawes was in the habit of beating his horses so unmercifully that finally one of the boys in the blacksmith shop threatened to beat him if he didn't stop, and his son, Walter Hawes, apparently fared no better than the horses. According to the same letter, every week when the old man came back on Saturday night from wherever it was that he had been whooping it up, he would put poor Walter through the same grim ritual. "Have you been a good boy?" he would ask, and "Yes, sir," Walter would say, but the boy's answer never satisfied him, and every week as regular as clockwork, he would take him out to the woods and whale the tar out of him. It got so bad that eventually the boys in his father's shop and some other friends chipped in to make up a purse that Walter could use to put as much distance between himself and his father as possible. He wound up in Cuba for a while and then returned as far as Boston, where he went into the machine business and made a pretty good thing of it by all accounts. He didn't come back to Shaftsbury for forty years, long after his father had gone on to his dubious reward, but his old friend Stephen A. Whipple recognized him immediately anyway because, as he wrote, "Few men had such a profile as he had." You can't help wishing that he had gone into detail.

If Silas Hawes was a tormentor of children and animals, he also had another string to his bow. He invented things. Again, you wish more details were available, but what few survive are fascinating. At some point in his life, for instance, he tried to construct a perpetual motion machine, and it is easy to picture him tinkering away after hours on some Rube Goldberg contraption of crazily balanced weights, gears, flywheels, and heaven only knows what all else, which would somehow manage to keep itself going forever. Maybe this was after young Walter had run off to Cuba, and what the old scoundrel was really trying to construct was a contraption to make him forget that he was the one who had driven him to it. There is no evidence that he ever succeeded, but there is no evidence that he failed either. How can you be sure about a man like Hawes? Perhaps in some dark place or forgotten corner—possibly somewhere in the old mill itself—there is still to be heard the dim rasp of metal against metal, like an old man's whisper, a queerly shaped shadow wheeling tirelessly around and around like the vicious circle of an old man's regrets.

Then he got another idea, which was in its way even more extraordinary and which it is hard not to associate with the mill, with the rush of Paran Creek, the flume, the millpond, all that water forever tumbling by. "Time like an ever rolling stream / Bears all its sons away," runs the hymn that the old sinner must have heard many a Sunday morning after beating the daylights out of Walter the night before, and you can imagine him putting it all together: time rolling by, the water rolling by, his boy gone downstream, whom in his lifetime he was never to lay eyes on again. It is as if Silas Hawes chose to see flux and change as the enemy instead of himself and wanted to stop them dead in their tracks before they stopped him dead in his—a perpetual halt this time instead of perpetual motion. So he conjured up the scheme of pressing the water into a solid form so you could cut it in slices like a cheese, thus stilling its babbling rehearsals of mortality and loss forever. Or maybe his motives were entirely commercial. What a killing a man might make, after all, if he could press the clear, fresh water of the millstream when it was plentiful in the spring and then sell it in the dog days when springs were drying up and wells starting to run low. Great wheels of water could be stored like wheels of cheddar or Stilton, and once you got the hang of it, there was no reason you couldn't turn out different kinds of water for different kinds of taste—water drawn off at night and pressed into molds with the moonlight still in it, water cold enough to make your teeth ache from April when the stream was swollen with melting snow. You could cut yourself a wedge as dark and still as the day it was dipped out through a hole in the ice with a wooden bucket, or sample another still warm and green from an August afternoon when the shafts of Shaftsbury sun were alive with midges and old Hawes dozed off with a fishpole across his knees.

But back to that day in 1812 when the peddler gave him the used saw blades in exchange for shoeing his horse. This time Hawes came through with an invention that was classic in its simplicity and could be used in an almost infinite number of ways, that was inexpensive and relatively uncomplicated to manufacture, and, above all, that worked. He took two of the blades, welded them together at right angles, and thus produced what seems to have been the first carpenter's square ever to have been made out of steel, either in this country or anywhere else. Up to this point, all such squares had evidently been made of wood held together at the angle with a piece of metal; although they worked well enough for ordinary carpentry, they did not hold up indefinitely and were especially unsuited for testing the squaring of hot-iron work at the blacksmith's forge. Hawes lost no time in taking out a patent on his brainchild, and in 1817 he and the previously mentioned Stephen Whipple, another Shaftsbury smith, went into the business of manufacturing them in quantity, all made, stamped, and graduated by hand. They went for anything from three to seven dollars apiece, which was quite a price for the time, but even so the demand grew at such an encouraging rate that Hawes and Whipple decided they needed more room for their operation. In 1823, on the same land where his house stood and still stands today, Stephen Whipple put up a three-story building with a trip hammer in it that was run by a waterwheel. On the ground floor the squares were made and the horses shod, and the upper two stories were used for grinding grain. And thus, at last, the Old Mill of Shaftsbury was born.

Whipple built his mill to last while he was at it, with walls some thirty inches thick made of local stone, and heavy, hand-hewn beams. It outlasted the three generations of Whipples who owned and operated it until it was finally sold out of the family in 1920 just short of a hundred years later and put to other uses altogether. There was a broad wooden ramp leading to the second floor so the farmers could drive their wagons up for loading and unloading. The bags of grain were hoisted up to the third floor by means of a chain attached to the extension of the gable, emptied into a chute for grinding between water-operated millstones on the way down, and then loaded back into the wagons again. Wheat, corn, rye, barley—you could bring your own grain and have it ground to your own specifications for cow feed or whatever, and if you didn't have grain of your own, you could buy it at the mill ready-ground. There were long sheds outside for the horses and of course no Routes 7 or 67 then, no railway overpass, no cars, no gas stations, just the grass and trees, a dirt road winding by, and the mill itself with its soft tan stonework, its high-pitched roof and deep-set windows, all of it reflected upside down in the pond. The rush of water over the dam, the creaking of harness and chain hoist, the voices of farmers, the clip-clop of hooves on hard-packed earth, and always from the smithy the clang and clatter of anvil and trip hammer turning out squares. All through the Middle West, from the opening of that territory until the Civil War, the steel squares were among the great building tools, and by 1828 Stephen Whipple's son Edward and his brother Angell were selling them to the men who were migrating still farther afield to the Northwest Territory. Later on, Edward settled in Illinois, and a steady stream of his father's product went out to him from the Shaftsbury mill.

Silas Hawes, in the meanwhile, had his troubles. For unknown reasons—to help finance some of his farther-fetched inventions maybe—he borrowed money from a missionary fund controlled by one Deacon Hindsill of North Bennington, and when he could not pay it back, Hindsill attached his patent and held it for a while. Then in the spring of 1825 Stephen Whipple and Garner Barton bought the land on which the Eagle Square Company now stands and put up some more buildings to make squares in. That November Hawes leased the buildings for ten years at an annual rent of $106. A few years later he retired from business and was heard of no more. His patent ran out eventually, and several other shops, including a couple in North Bennington, started getting into the act too. It was Whipple and Barton, however, who prevailed, eventually putting the competition out of business entirely. Their success has been attributed chiefly to a man named Norman Millington, who in 1854 invented a device for mechanically cutting the graduation marks in the squares. Before this, the cutting had been done by hand, which meant that for a square marked off in eighths of inches, you had to cut as many as twelve hundred graduations, one at a time. Millington's machine could do twenty-four in a single operation.

Having made good in Boston by this time and finally returned home to Shaftsbury, Walter Hawes was the one who, around 1860, suggested the name "Eagle," by which it is known still. As an old man, Stephen Whipple sold out to three men who built a factory about a quarter of a mile downstream of the mill, and that is where the Eagle Square Company still stands. In 1864 the company changed from a partnership to a stock corporation, and one of its directors and the holder of 25 percent of its stock was a Massachusetts congressman during Lincoln's administration named Oakes Ames, who later became deeply implicated in the Crédit Mobilier railroad scandal, the Watergate of its day, and was censured by the House. From the mill as a hub, the spokes go out in all directions.

After his retirement, Stephen Whipple continued to live in the house that he had built across the pond from the mill, and there it was that he finally died in 1879 at the age of ninety-seven. He had been born in Cheshire, Massachusetts, in 1781, the tenth child of a shoemaker and his wife, and at the age of eighteen he went to learn the blacksmith trade from his older brother Oliver, who had a forge in Shaftsbury. In 1810 he married a Bennington girl named Louisa Edgerton, and in 1813 he built his house, which is thus ten years older then the mill. It was his son, Stephen A. Whipple, who took the business over when he finally bowed out.

There is a photograph of Stephen A. Whipple and his family all done up in their Sunday best. Stephen is wearing a coat that looks several sizes too big for him and is holding the youngest child on his knee. Beside him his wife, who was born Eliza Hicks, looks hollow-cheeked and older than Stephen with her hair skinned back into a bun and surrounded by enough children to make anybody's cheeks look hollow. Some letters survive from this period, and in one of them, dated June 10, 1843, her sister Jane writes of a recent change of pace in Manchester. "I was interrupted last evening," she says, "by a loud rap at the door. Father went to the door and a gentleman came in and said you will not turn a man out of doors such a night as this. Father told him no. He said he had a load in his wagon. They drove around to the shed. They came in. It was Mr. Van Housen with a black man, his wife, and three children escaping from slavery. They stayed until morning, the handsomest *Negro* we have ever seen."

The tradition is that ten years later, in 1852, there was a fire in the mill, but the newspapers of this period are missing from the *Bennington Banner* files, and no details are remembered. Presumably the damage was not great, however, because in 1856 the mill was back in business again. In 1883 the blacksmith shop on the ground floor was given up. After Stephen A. Whipple, it was his son Will who carried on until he closed the mill down for good in 1917.

In the same photograph mentioned above, Will appears as a boy of thirteen or fourteen sitting beside his mother, Eliza, with his hands folded on his lap, his bow tie on crooked, and looking as though he is awaiting execution. There is also another photograph taken perhaps sixty or seventy years later that shows him as an old man with his execution a much more imminent reality. In that one Will Whipple is sitting propped up in a high-backed wooden chair with a pillow behind him and a cane in each hand. His right leg is stretched out stiffly in front of him. The chair has been set out on the lawn, and you can see a tree and a stretch of dirt road in the background. They could not get him to put on his Sunday best this time. Instead, he wears the same kind of work shirt and overalls that he must have worn all those years as a miller. But he has let them brush his hair and part it anyhow, and there is a formal look about him the way he sits there facing the camera just as squarely and unenthusiastically as he faced it as a boy many years before. They have placed him looking directly into the sun, but he is not squinting. His jaw is set firm under the shadow of his white mustache, and he is staring straight into the camera. He hasn't got much time left, and he knows it, but what he still has he is prepared to make the best of with those two skinny canes and his one good leg to help him.

This is Will Whipple more or less the way Anson Hawkins remembers him from his boyhood. The old man spent a fair amount of time with him in those days, used to help him fish for trout in the millpond and let him keep them alive in big iron pot full of rainwater he had outside. It has been reported that Will Whipple had a good sense of humor, but Anson Hawkins says he would be no judge of that. He knew Mr. Whipple the way a small boy is apt to know an old man. For old men and small boys both, summers tend to drag after a while, and finding ways to liven them up a little was a serious business. There was never much time for kidding around.

Generally speaking, however, Will Whipple never won any popularity contests among the young, Anson Hawkins's relationship with him notwithstanding. He put in a lot of work on his lawn and his flowers, and when boys came climbing his high fence to look for baseballs struck over it from the school diamond on the other side, it drove him wild. He used to stand out there during recess time with a very unsentimental look in his eyes. He had one finger missing for some reason, and Anson Hawkins remembers that the way you might expect a small boy would. He remembers Will said he tried to get a doctor to sew it back on for him when he first lost it, but the doctor told him he'd come too late.

Hawkins also remembers the mill in operation back in Will Whipple's time, how the largest part of what they ground came down on the Bennington and Rutland Railroad from a Rutland wholesaler to be unloaded at the South Shaftsbury depot. There it was reloaded at a siding only five hundred yards from the mill and drawn the rest of the way by horse. The corn came loose, but the oats, barley, wheat, and so on to mix it with were in sacks. He remembers the separate hoppers the different grains were stored in.

At some point after the mill closed in 1917, it was sold to Charles Graves, and from then until 1925 it seems to have been more or less abandoned. Occasionally water seeped into the ground floor where the blacksmith shop had been, and a family or two of rats moved in. In summertime, kids would come to swim in the pond, and the abandoned old building was where they changed their clothes. In spite of the rats, the girls used the ground floor, where Silas Hawes may once have worked on his perpetual motion machine, and the boys used the second, where the freshly ground grain used to fall down the chute to be bagged. Anson Hawkins says the boys had a hole that they used to check on the girls through. Maybe the girls had one too that he didn't know about. In any case, all of this came to an end finally with the arrival of a maiden lady from La Crosse, Wisconsin, who would have been scandalized by such goings-on and who, in 1925, bought the old place and restored it to respectability.

Her name was Anne Edwards, and to add yet another spoke heading off in yet another direction, one of her forebears was

Jonathan Edwards, the great Puritan divine, revivalist, and president of Princeton University, who died of an unsuccessful smallpox inoculation about twenty years before the first Stephen Whipple was born. Miss Edwards was born in 1879, which made her forty-six when she came to Shaftsbury. She was a rather formidable lady with long, dark hair, which, like Eliza Whipple before her, she combed back into a bun. A graduate of Wellesley, she had worked in Boston as a librarian for a while and also for a time was secretary to Katherine Lee Bates, who wrote "America the Beautiful." Another spoke. She had inherited some money from her father, which she invested so shrewdly that it wasn't long before her income made it unnecessary to have a job. The story was that she had had a suitor once when she was younger, but he was a Roman Catholic and she had strong views, and so it came to nothing. Instead she had a number of "very sincere lady friends," as her niece Posy described them, and she also had a dog named Michael, who was her love and her despair.

In the summer of 1924 she rented a house in Dorset, a town a little north of Shaftsbury, with the idea of scouting around to find a place where she could settle down permanently. In addition to her two sisters, she had a young niece with her—Kathryn Edwards, nicknamed Posy—and the four of them spent a lot of time exploring the countryside north of Dorset but turning up nothing that struck Miss Edwards's fancy. It was not until the fall, after Posy had gone back to La Crosse to finish her last two years of high school, that Miss Edwards started exploring in a southerly direction, and it was in Shaftsbury, of course, that her fancy was struck a blow from which it never fully recovered.

There it stood, one hundred and one years after Stephen Whipple had built it. The roof had partly fallen in. The windows were smashed. The horse sheds were in ruins. There was water trickling in periodically, not to mention the rats. But the old stonework had mellowed with age. It was all shades of moth brown and dove gray by now. A century of weather had softened all the angles and corners, and smoke from the forge had darkened the great beams. Beside that, there was the haze of autumn in the air, the gold and scarlet leaves floating in the dark water of the pond. There were the tall elms, the little bridge. Miss Edwards knew her search had ended. The old spinster had lost her heart at last.

By the following July, once the sale was completed and the deed signed, she was ready to get down to work. She had the stone walls of the flume reinforced and the dam rebuilt, both to make them more sightly and to make sure she wouldn't be flooded out when the waters rose. She also rebuilt the terrace that juts out into the pond and added a screened porch in the back where you have to raise your voice to be heard above the sound of the millstream rushing by. She had several rustic bridges built, had the horse sheds torn down, and added a low ell to make room for the kitchen, the furnace room, and an attached garage. For the stone that was needed for all this she saw to it that the same old quarry was used from which the original stone had come, and when the $5000 she had allocated to this ran out, she made sure that the stucco they finished the job with was a good match. Where the wagon ramp to the second floor had been, she put in a concrete stairway. All of this was just the outside work.

On the inside she turned the ground floor into a single, large, meandering room full of unexpected corners, alcoves, and angles. It was a combination of living room, dining room, library, and study, with parts of it always beyond the reach of the sunlight that comes in through the deeply recessed windows in those almost three-feet-thick walls. Those windows presented the good lady with a special problem because, although at first glance the openings seemed to be uniform, they turned out not to be, and each one had to be fitted with a casement of a different size. She left the old smoke-stained beams exposed and kept the stone floor. Making use of the chimney that had been employed in connection with the forge, she had an enormous stone fireplace built out from the wall, and behind it is the shadowiest of the little rooms within a room. Most inspired of all, perhaps, is the hanging stairway of white reinforced concrete that leads to the second story. It is semicircular in shape and delicate as the whorl of a seashell as it curves its way up to the landing above. Beneath the curve of its underside is another of the rooms within a room, this one usually bright with sun. A friend of Posy's sister Eleanor published a murder mystery set in the old mill, and it was at the bottom of this stairway that the body of rich old Aunt Geraldine Harcourt was found. It is just as well that rich old Aunt Anne Edwards didn't live to read it. The author, who was also a ghost writer for Eleanor Roosevelt, described the room as full of shadows, and so it is. But it is full of sun too, shadows and sunbeams existing side by side in curious harmony. Because of the thick walls it is as cool as a cave even on the hottest summer days, and because of them too it is full of silence even now when all the traffic and turmoil of Route 7 have replaced the inconspicuous dirt road that was there when Miss Edwards moved in in 1925. Beyond its walls it is the 1990s with a vengeance, but inside it is still seventy years ago and earlier. Silas Hawes would hear nothing to puzzle him if he came back some night to hammer out a square of two, and if he stepped out back to check on the perpetual motion of the stars, the roar of the millstream would still drown out all other sounds just about the way it did in his day.

On the second floor Miss Edwards divided the one big room where the grain had been ground into three bedrooms and a bath, but the third floor, reached by an almost vertical wooden stair, she left much as it was, with the heavy rafters and high-pitched roof. The door is still there that the grain used to be hoisted through from wagons below, with one window above it and another on either side. It is one of the snuggest, most enchanted parts of the house, way up there under the gable looking out at the sky and the tops of trees, a wonderful place to read a book or write one, to paint a picture or take a nap or listen to the rain on the slate roof. Miss Edwards stored things up there as time went by, and many of them are still around—humpbacked trunks full of old clothes, old letters, hatboxes, photograph albums, magazines, the usual debris of the years.

Among them are some diaries she kept in a rather haphazard way from time to time, including the one that she started on January 2, 1926, only a few days after she first moved in at Christmastime. It tells a good deal both about the things that happened and about the lady they happened to.

"The year opens at the Mill with confusion, disorder, and dirt in command," she writes in her sensible, up-and-down script. "But I am living here! Almost unrealizable, almost an occasion for awe. At present my thoughts revert often to Samuel Pepys, who in his famous diary somewhere remarks, 'I have bought me a new coat, and now I pray that the good Lord will make me able to pay for it.' So may some miraculous power enable me to pay for my house. This is written on January 2, not first. Cause—the furnace fire on Jan. 1 evening went out, and I spent from 12 to 2 coaxing it back to life. The first day's experimenting with coke."

She also had trouble with her dog, Michael, those first days and wrote, "He wants to run, run anywhere but over his own 14 acres.

And he is as easy to catch as a bird. I am learning all the dirty back yards in the village. Perhaps that is their attraction for M. I'll try it a few days more and if I don't learn him nothing [you can see the corners of her mouth curl as she sets down that venture into the vernacular without quotation marks, the old Wellesley grad] I shall have to dispose of him." A threat that is unlikely to have caused Michael much loss of sleep.

She was an old maid, and she liked things tidy. When she discovered that the reason the rugs wouldn't lie straight was that the stairway was uneven and the chimney not square, she snorted, "A fine job!" and then added a word or two on mankind in general and the Shaftsbury variety in particular. "They are all tricky and ready to take advantage of anyone they can—like myself." But she had her good moments too. She took long walks along "my brook, which surprised me by being deep and swift and rushing. Many swimming holes. One spot where the sheep were always taken to be washed. Fine stinging air and Michael and I much enjoyed it." And later, on January 9, "the first real snow storm and how I loved it—several inches on the ground when I woke and more coming. Enjoyed my shoveling. The snow was light and feathery. Michael was enchanted."

There were neighbors whom she was less than enthusiastic about—some of them stayed too long when they came to call, others were know-it-alls. But some of them became good friends, like Mr. Monroe, who came to her rescue on the fateful night of January 18 when, after a thaw and a heavy rain, she was treated to her first flood. It occasioned the longest and most impassioned entry she wrote. The brook turned into a raging torrent. The water rose to within inches of the top of the dam and finally welled up into the furnace room where it poured through the coke pile in a thick, black stream. For a while she had to bale the place out by herself, carrying one bucket at a time up the steep stairs, but finally Mr. Monroe arrived in rubber boots and dungarees, and they worked together steadily until two o'clock in the morning with only a quick break for a snack at midnight. By morning the worst was over, but it took all day for the millstream to subside. She ends her account with a scathing denunciation of the local contractor, who she felt was responsible for the leak in the furnace room; "I want to record Mr. ——'s helpfulness!" she writes, the point of her pencil almost breaking off. The strain was apparently too much for her because it is the last entry for the year.

In 1934 she tried the diary again, but like its predecessor, it is only a few pages long. Friends came to visit and neighbors to have supper. She took walks with the indefatigable Michael, went shopping in Bennington and Troy, had more trouble from the furnace and letters from her niece Posy, who, after the death of her mother in 1926, made the mill her home when she wasn't away at the Northampton School for Girls or Mount Holyoke. On Tuesday, February 13, Miss Edwards wrote only four words: "The day Michael died." The rest of the diary is nothing but empty pages.

But it was by no means an empty life if outwardly not an especially eventful one. Her major accomplishment, of course, was the mill—discovering it the way she did that Dorset summer, buying it, restoring it to life. She never tried to make it look prettier or quainter than it already was, but in everything she did always respected the stoneness and squareness and Whippleness of the place. The third floor is marvelous because she left it marvelously the way it always had been, and the great room downstairs is a masterpiece because although, with the kind of taste that is so good you don't notice it, she transformed it from a blacksmith shop into a wonderfully civilized, imaginative, un-chintzy living room and then some, it wouldn't take Stephen Whipple twenty-four hours to turn it back into a blacksmith shop again. She also took an active interest in community affairs and local politics, and the same sense of tidiness that led her to excoriate the Shaftsbury workmen for those rugs that wouldn't lie straight persuaded her to found the first official town dump. All in all she lived at the mill thirty years before she was through, and somewhere along the line a friend who signed herself or himself only as M.K.C. wrote a poem about her and the mill that contains such lines as these:

> A warmth of spirit and of soul burn here
> Haunting the farthest reaches of the house.
> Outside there is the dignity of trees,
> The green perfection of broad lawns and shrubs,
> The quiet of the millpond pool, the rush,
> The never ending sound of water fall.
> Here too is evidence of warmth and love,
> Of self submerged in larger, richer life.

At least M.K.C. felt that way, and there are people in Shaftsbury still who would agree. In 1955 Miss Edwards died at the mill at the age of seventy-six and left a large portion of her estate to found a humane society for dogs and cats. It is no great mystery why. That same year the mill was bought from the estate by her niece Posy, who was by then Mrs. Gerhard Gerlach, but to explain how that came about, it is necessary to go back a few years.

As already noted, after the death of her mother, Posy Edwards made the mill her home, and what she remembered best from those first years was the fun she had there. She was a pretty little bit of a person with dark hair and fierce dark eyes and an angle to her jaw that made you think twice about crossing her. She was full of bounce, with an abrupt, peppery way of saying just what she felt like saying, no more and no less, and a quick little laugh that went off like a string of Chinese crackers when you least expected it. She loved good times and had a way of making them happen around her, with classmates from Mount Holyoke accompanying her home and friends dropping in from Bennington and Shaftsbury and towns round about. They had Christmas parties and picnics and dances. They had swimming in the millpond and sunbathing on the terrace, which Aunt Anne Edwards didn't approve of one bit—"Bodies are ugly!" she said—but they kept on doing it anyway because Aunt Anne had a soft spot for Posy.

She built her a tennis court one summer out past where the horse sheds had been, letting the Shaftsbury young come play there too as long as they were decently clothed. But then in 1929 Posy got restless. She decided to visit her sister Eleanor in Paris, where she was living with her new English husband, whom Posy had never met.

Much as Aunt Anne had fallen in love with the mill, so Posy fell in love with Paris. Eleanor persuaded her that since she was a French major anyway, it would make perfect sense to stay on for a while and take courses at the Sorbonne and the Alliance Française, which she did. Eleanor seems to have had a special flair for arranging her younger sister's life. It wasn't long afterward that she told her she ought to find something to do with her hands as well as her brain, and what she decided to do, because she had a friend who was involved, was to take up bookbinding. It proved a fateful decision. Her second year in Paris she gave up her French studies in order to study binding full time. After seeing a wonderful exhibit of hand bindings at the Petit Palais, the best of which were the work of the great German binder Ignatz Wiemler, she decided to continue her studies at the State Academy of Graphic Arts in Leipzig, where Wiemler taught. Sewing and pasting, skiving leather, making headbands, applying gold leaf, tooling in gold and tooling blind, setting type to stamp titles—all such basic techniques of binding and more were in the curriculum, and her letters back to Aunt Anne at the mill are full of detail. Eventually another detail crept in. There was a young man she started having noon coffee breaks with named Gerhard Gerlach, a native of Schweidnitz, in Silesia, who was Wiemler's star student. Since neither of them spoke the other's language, Posy took a Berlitz course in German and after two years of bookbinding in Leipzig could handle it pretty well. By this time she and Gerhard had very little trouble communicating.

In August 1933, she returned to the United States, and after a stay with Aunt Anne in Shaftsbury went down to New York to investigate the possibilities of earning a living as a bookbinder. She finally turned up a job teaching the subject as occupational therapy at a sanitarium in Connecticut. The salary was meager, but she was given a nice little house to live in. By Christmas she decided she could live no longer without Gerhard, so back she sailed for Germany and persuaded him to return with her in the hope that he could join her in her teaching at the sanitarium. When this fell through, Posy's Aunt Helen Edwards, Aunt Anne's sister, invited the two of them to live with her as chaperone in a small apartment in New York, and it was there that they first set themselves up as binders. It was there also that Gerhard, who weighed only 125 when he first came over, put on 20 pounds after just six months of Aunt Helen's cooking. Brought up in Germany during the hungry days of the First World War, he spent the rest his life making up for it. He loved raising garden plants, but exclusively the edible kind. He took care of the vegetables and left the posies to Posy.

One thing led to another, and through the friendship of Christopher Lehmann-Haupt, the librarian at Columbia University, Posy and Gerhard were invited to teach bookbinding there in the fall. With the assurance of a steady income at last, they were able to get married, and the ceremony took place on July 21, 1934, at the First Church in Old Bennington, that most beautiful of all New England churches, with its snow-white box pews and the twin stairways that lead up to the high pulpit. The reception took place in the garden of the mill afterward. Aunt Anne was a fire-breathing teetotaler so that was that. But one of Posy's brothers smuggled in a bottle of champagne and another of burgundy, so when Miss Edwards was looking the other way, the thirty-odd guests had a chance to sneak at least a token toast to the bride and groom.

For twenty-five years they taught binding at Columbia, and it was during this period that two children were born—a son, Teddy, who was killed in a motorcycle accident when he was seventeen, and a daughter, Kathryn, who was eventually married out of the mill like her mother before her. At Columbia the Gerlachs's students numbered more than a thousand and included librarians, commercial binders who wanted to learn hand binding, inexperienced binders who wanted to improve their technique, and a whole assortment of others who took it up just for the fun of it—fat ones and thin ones, deft ones and clumsy ones, old ones and young ones, all of them losing themselves in the endless details and infinite pains necessary to bind from scratch or to restore a book to the Gerlachs's high standards. In addition, they gave private lessons in their own bindery—first at the Japan Paper Company in New York and later in Chappaqua—and also bound books to order. It was with these latter books, of course, that their real craftsmanship and artistry came into play, and before they were done, they won international recognition.

When Bruce Rogers printed his great lectern Bible for the coronation of Edward VIII, he was so impressed by their work that he had them bind a number of copies including the one in the University Chapel at Princeton, where Posy's ancestor Jonathan Edwards had taken that fatal inoculation. They bound a whole edition of memorial volumes for old John D. Rockefeller and were all set to bind copies of John F. Kennedy's inaugural address for distribution to his friends when the young president decided that it might seem presumptuous of him and canceled the arrangement. Publishers commissioned them to bind special presentation copies of books by their favorite authors, like John Steinbeck, Nicholas Murray Butler, Generals Marshall and Eisenhower, and others.

The playwright Arthur Miller was so delighted by a special binding they did for him that he commissioned them to do another for Marilyn Monroe, who was then his wife, and Gerhard really threw himself into that one. He made a special box for it lined with voluptuous blue-green silk and covered the book itself in soft, blush-pink leather with a pair of little red dots abreast, so to speak, on the front cover. Miss Edwards had no use for Germans and made no bones about it, but she made an exception in Gerhard's case because he was the only man she knew who could make her laugh till she cried. He seems to have had a way with people in general—a habit of really listening to who they were as well as to what they said, which tended to blow away like chaff all the barriers between Shaftsbury and Schweidnitz.

And of course there was the business of restoration—taking priceless and irreplaceable old fifteenth-, sixteenth-, seventeenth-century volumes with their spines broken, their joints cracked, their leather dry and crumbling, their pages damp-stained and brittle, and putting them back in shape with such skill that often it would take an expert's eye to know they had been tampered with. This was the meticulous kind of work that Posy excelled in, always insisting that although Gerhard was equally good at it, he, unlike her, was an artist as well—a poet in leather, a painter in calfskin and gold. They were both masters of their craft, and both, in their own ways, artists of such note that no history of American binding can be complete without them.

Then, in 1955, Aunt Anne Edwards died, and, as they had always hoped they might, Posy and Gerhard Gerlach bought the mill from her estate, although they were not to move in right away. For seven years they lived on in Chappaqua and rented the mill out winters to various tenants including the wife of a former president of Bennington College and the novelist Bernard Malamud and his wife, who never actually moved in because they decided that the noise of the water was too distracting. By way of a footnote, it might be added that back in Miss Edwards's time there was another distinguished person who might have lived in the mill but never quite made it. As Posy told it, Miss Edwards returned from shopping one day to find that a strange woman had let herself in and was sitting waiting for her in the living room. The woman said she admired the mill from the road and would like to rent it. Miss Edwards's response to this assault on her privacy was instantaneous. "Get out!" she said with terrible clarity. It was not until later that she found out from a newspaper photograph that the woman was Katharine Hepburn, but the chances are that she would have responded no differently if she had recognized her in the first place.

During those first seven years, the Gerlachs themselves came up only for vacations during the summer, when they would roll back Miss Edwards's oriental rugs on the ground floor and give polka parties till Stephen Whipple's rafters rang as they hadn't rung since trip-hammer days. It was not until 1962 that they left Chappaqua and, with all their equipment, moved into the mill for good.

They renovated and extended the garage that Miss Edwards had added and made it into a bindery large enough to hold all the magnificent apparatus, gadgetry, and impedimenta of their craft. Silas Hawes would have gone green with envy—the guillotine for trimming edges, the great table shears with their blades ajar like the beaks of pterodactyls, the tall press for stamping titles in gold, silver, or anything else a customer might require, the sewing frames, the medieval-looking book presses with their heavy iron wheels as big around as any wheel of water old Hawes ever dreamed of turning out. Add to that cabinets full of gorgeous endpapers, marbled, paisleyed, flowered like the shawls of kings; the leathers of every kind from Germany, France, England, Morocco; the racks of brass tooling wheels and hand stamps in every shape imaginable, including stars and crowns, pomegranates, fleurs-de-lis, heraldic beasts. Gerhard spared no expense to make his work perfect, and if he didn't have the stamp you wanted, he would have one specially made. The Gerlachs were back in business again, and once more the work came pouring in.

In 1964 their daughter Kathryn gave them a surprise party for their thirtieth wedding anniversary, with swimming in the pond and Japanese lanterns strung around out back where some of the old mill machinery still stands under cover. Friends came from all over creation bringing good things to eat and things to drink that would have driven Miss Edwards up the wall if she had happened by. What was a surprise even to Kathryn was that it was almost two days before the last guests tottered home.

Four years later, Gerhard died of heart disease, but Posy stayed on until her own death more than twenty years later, practicing the same kind of wizardry—binding, restoring, teaching other people how. Her eyes remained dark and fierce till the end, the line of her jaw dangerous, and her laugh as quick as the flicker of her hands when she was putting the finishing touches on a book that would have made even the great Wiemler himself sit up and take notice. The Gerlachs's daughter, Kathryn, lives there till this day.

So there they all are. Silas Hawes, that old lunatic, tyrant, genius. And the three generations of Whipples—the first Stephen, who recorded his father's memories of how Walter Hawes was driven beyond endurance and fled to Cuba; and Stephen, his son; and Will, his grandson, old Will, who let them prop him up in the sunshine to have his picture taken with a pair of canes. And the rats. And the young Shaftsbury bucks peering down through a hole in the floor at the young Shaftsbury belles. And Miss Edwards tapping her foot when the neighbors overstayed their welcome; and walking her Michael through the feathery snow; and while the waters rose outside, having that harried snack with Mr. Monroe, who was possibly the only gentleman she ever shared a midnight with. And then the Gerlachs moving in with their bindery and completing the circle by bringing back a venerable handicraft to the mill. It had been built for such work in the first place, after all.

And that is just the inner circle, the hub, from which all the spokes radiate out as far as the eye can see and farther than that if you feel like looking farther. Crédit Mobilier. America the Beautiful. Marilyn Monroe and Eleanor Roosevelt. A black man and his family running for their lives. Myself, who am both the author of these words and a former student of the great Posy's. And whoever you are who is reading this. Generally speaking, the threads that bind us to each other are no less real for being mostly invisible, no less important and precious. In the long run, each of our stories turns out to be the story of us all, and the home we long for has in all likelihood been home to others whose names we don't even know and will be home again to still others when the ever-rolling stream of things has long since borne us away.

6

◇ ◇ ◇ ◇ ◇

The Journey Toward Wholeness

Like the majority of humankind I don't know much about wholeness at first hand. It is something that, at most—like Abraham and Sarah and Moses and the rest of them—I have every once in a while seen and greeted from afar, as the author of the Letter to the Hebrews puts it, but that is about all. I like to believe that in a disorganized way it is what I am journeying toward, but the most I have to show for my pains is an occasional glimpse of it in certain people who had clay feet more or less like the rest of us but who struck me as being at least a good deal wholer than I have ever managed to become myself. I think particularly of my maternal grandmother, whom as a child I named Naya for some forgotten reason, so let me start with her.

Naya was born in Washington, D.C., two years after the assassination of Abraham Lincoln and lived well into her nineties. Like everybody else, she had her happy times and her sad times, her weaknesses and her strengths, her good luck and her bad luck, but what made her unique in my experience was that no matter what happened to her, she seemed always remarkably and invincibly herself. Even when her life was shattered by the deaths of people she loved and by other kinds of loss or failure, she remained so serene and intact that it was as if she lived out of some deep center within herself that was beyond the reach of circumstance. My clearest memory of her is in a white linen dress sitting on a terrace among the Blue Ridge Mountains in Tryon, North Carolina, reading a yellow-backed French novel and smoking a Chesterfield in a white paper cigarette holder. My grandfather had lost most of his money by then, and they had had to move away from the place where they had lived for many years, leaving all their old friends and their old life behind them, but as far as I could see it never caused her to turn a hair. She found new friends and a new life and made do on what money they still had, saying only that she wished she had spent more of it on herself because then she would at least have had something left to show for it. She was entirely Naya still, as much the same person she had always been as the mountains around her were the same mountains, and when she was already an old lady and I was still a boy, we drew up a list of most of the people we knew which we entitled "Tryon Crackpots, amiable and otherwise, by two of their number." We did not for one moment believe that we were crackpots ourselves but added that part in hopes that if the list ever fell into the wrong hands, the note of humility might save us.

I remember her again some twenty years later lying in her bed in a nursing home within a few months of her death in 1961, by which time she was in her ninety-fourth year and too old and frail with a broken hip to live anywhere else but intact in every other way. My wife and I drove down from New Hampshire to see her there with our two-year-old daughter, Katherine, in tow, and when we got home, she wrote a letter to thank us. Her handwriting had gone loose and spidery by then, but with effort it is still possible to read it. "Dear children," she wrote, "it was a noble deed to make the long journey down here, and the joy of seeing you and your bewitching little fairy daughter more than compensated me for the ignominy of substituting an old crone in a dark little room for the Naya of legend. Tell Katherine not to forget my dimple [Katherine had the same little star-shaped mark on her hand that Naya did] and how is Dinah's German accent [we had left our middle daughter, Dinah, in the care of a German au pair girl]? Many thanks and much love, Naya." It was the last letter we ever had from her.

She was indeed an old crone in a dark little room as she said, but because she knew she was, because she could see clearly and without either bitterness or complaint that that was what the years had reduced her to, because there was something in her that was half amused at the sight and to that extent untouched by it, she was of course a good deal more than that too. There was a room inside her which was neither dark nor little, and in that room she continued to be—how to put words to it without tarnishing it?—full of wit and eloquence to the end. It is a glimpse of at least some important aspect of wholeness that I carry with me to this day, a bit of banister to hold onto as I prepare, myself, to climb the dark stair.

Naya saw herself clearly in the nursing home, but she saw my wife and me and our small blonde child clearly too. That was another part of her wholeness. She knew as well as I did that in all likelihood it was the last time we would ever see each other, as indeed it turned out to be, but there was no sentimentality in her at that final meeting. I do not think I have ever known anybody as unsentimental. She was never a hugging, kissing kind of grandmother, and I cannot remember ever seeing her cry. One Christmas I gave her a tattered copy of a long out-of-print novel by Jean Ingelow called *Fated to Be Free,* which she had loved as a young woman and hadn't seen since, and when she opened the package and discovered what it was, the sheer surprise of it made her voice falter for a moment and tears come to her eyes, but that is the closest I ever saw her come to it. When we sentimentalize about things, we see not so much the things themselves as we see the flood of feeling, of sentiment, that the things occasion in us, with the result that sentimentality becomes a form of blocking out the world. But Naya did not block out the world. It was not the flood of her own feeling that she saw that day. Instead she saw my wife and me and our daughter, and when she wrote of the "joy" of the occasion, I do not think she was exaggerating. I think that the sight of youth and life in the dark little room rejoiced her spirit in a way that was undimmed by the fact, which she also saw, that she was herself old and close to her life's end. She did not lose sight of us by focusing on her own predicament, as I am quite sure that in her place I would have done. Instead it would be more accurate to say that she lost sight of her own predicament by focusing on us, and I believe that the capacity for doing that is another mark of her wholeness.

To be whole, I think, means among other things that you see the world whole. She wrote of the ignominy of having become an old woman in a nursing home instead of the Naya of legend, but because she was able not only to identify the ignominy but also not to be overwhelmed by it, she revealed herself as still the Naya of legend even so. At the same time she identified what she called the joy of seeing us without being overwhelmed by that either, over-whelmed, that is, in the sense of losing track of the joy in the real-ization that she was never going to experience it again. In other words, she was "all there," as the saying goes. She saw both the light and the dark of what the world was offering her and was not split in two by them. She was whole in herself and she saw the world whole.

The world floods in on all of us. The world can be kind, and it can be cruel. It can be beautiful, and it can be appalling. It can give us good reason to hope and good reason to give up all hope. It can strengthen our faith in a loving God, and it can decimate our faith. In our lives in the world, the temptation is always to go where the world takes us, to drift with whatever current happens to be run-ning strongest. When good things happen, we rise to heaven; when bad things happen, we descend to hell. When the world strikes out at us, we strike back, and when one way or another the world blesses us, our spirits soar. I know this to be true of no one as well as I know it to be true of myself. I know how just the weather can affect my whole state of mind for good or ill, how just getting stuck in a traffic jam can ruin an afternoon that in every other way is so beautiful that it dazzles the heart. We are in constant danger of being not actors in the drama of our own lives but reactors. The fragmentary nature of our experience shatters us into fragments. Instead of being whole, most of the time we are in pieces, and we see the world in pieces, full of darkness at one moment and full of light the next.

It is in Jesus, of course, and in the people whose lives have been deeply touched by Jesus, and in ourselves at those moments when we also are deeply touched by him, that we see another way of

Peace I leave with you.

being human in this world, which is the way of wholeness. When we glimpse that wholeness in others, we recognize it immediately for what it is, and the reason we recognize it, I believe, is that no matter how much the world shatters us to pieces, we carry inside us a *vision* of wholeness that we sense is our true home and that beckons to us. It is part of what the book of Genesis means by saying that we are made in the image of God. It is part of what Saint Paul means by saying that the deepest undercurrent of all creation is the current that seeks to draw us toward what he calls mature humanhood, to the measure of the stature of the fullness of Christ.

I picture Jesus at the Last Supper when he had every reason to understand that the end was upon him—not as an old crone in a dark little room saying good-bye to her grandson and his family but as a young man in a dark little room saying good-bye to life itself and everything he had lived for and was prepared to die for. I picture him looking around at the twelve friends and making an unforgettable utterance. "Peace I leave with you," he says, when you would have thought he had no peace at all anywhere. "My peace I give to you; not as the world gives do I give to you. Let not your hearts be troubled, neither let them be afraid" (John 14:27).

The kind of peace that the world gives is the peace we experience when for a little time the world happens to be peaceful. It is a peace that lasts for only as long as the peaceful time lasts because as soon as the peaceful time ends, the peace ends with it. The peace that Jesus offers, on the other hand, has nothing to do with the things that are going on at the moment he offers it, which are for the most part tragic and terrible things. It is a peace beyond the reach of the tragic and terrible. It is a profound and inward peace that sees with unflinching clarity the tragic and terrible things that are happening and yet is not shattered by them. He loves his friends enough to be more concerned for their frightened and troubled hearts than he is for his own, and yet his love for his friends is no more where his peace comes from than his impending torture and death are where his peace will be destroyed. His peace comes not from the world but from something whole and holy within himself which sees the world also as whole and holy because deep beneath all the broken and unholy things that are happening in it even as he speaks, Jesus sees what he calls the Kingdom of God.

All his life long, wherever Jesus looked, he saw the world not in terms simply of its brokenness—a patchwork of light and dark calling forth in us now our light, now our dark—but in terms of the ultimate mystery of God's presence buried in it like a treasure buried in a field. It is not just that the Kingdom is *like* a pearl of great price, like a mustard seed, like leaven. It is indeed like them in ways that Jesus suggests in his parables, but it is also *within* them as it is also within us. Pearls, seeds, fields, leaven, the human heart, all of them carry within them something of the holiness of their origin. It is the wholest and realest part of their reality and of ours. Sinners are made in the image of God no less than saints. Even a sparrow fallen dead by the roadside is transparent to holiness. To be whole, I believe, is to see the world like that. To see the world like that, as Jesus saw it, is to be whole. And sometimes I believe that even people like you and me see it like that. Sometimes even in the midst of our confused and broken relationships with ourselves, with each other, with God, we catch glimpses of that holiness and wholeness which, no matter how buried and unrecognized, are still part of who we are.

Several summers ago I was driving to Pennsylvania for a speaking engagement. It was a beautiful day, and I wanted to make the most of the long trip by myself, wanted to be a as fully *present* in it as I could without letting my mind go off on a thousand different tangents. Hard as I tried to center myself, however, it didn't work very well. My scattered thoughts kept jerking me now this way, now that way, like a dog on a leash. I thought about the past. I thought about the future. I thought about other places, other times, about the group I was driving to Pennsylvania to talk to and what I was going to say to them when I got there. And then suddenly I started noticing the trees.

They were in full summer foliage. They were greener than I could remember ever having seen trees before. The sun was in them. The air was stirring them. As I drove by, they waved their leafy branches at me like plumes. They beckoned. They reached out. It was the wind, of course, that made them wave. It was the air whipped up by my car streaking by at sixty-five miles per hour. But no matter. They waved in the only way trees have of waving and caught my attention so completely that all other thoughts vanished from my head including my thoughts about them. I didn't think about them. I just saw them. I put no words to what was happening. I just let it happen. I just happened with it. Not until I got where I was going did I try to describe it.

The trees are always so glad to see us. That was the best way I could find to say it. They waved their branches like flags in a parade, haling me as I passed by as though I was some mighty spirit. They looked as if they had lined up for miles along the New York Thruway to greet me, and after a while I started waving back at them from time to time as if they too were mighty spirits and it was I who was greeting them. I believe I was not just being eccentric. I believe that for a little while I saw those trees as so real that I was myself made real by them. We were concentric. It was the whole of me that waved at the whole of them. There was no part of me left over to be anywhere other than where I was or to do anything other than what I was doing. And it was the same with the trees. The holiness that we shared—what it was that we were haling and honoring in each other—was that it was God who had formed and given life to us both. Trees and humans together, we had both proceeded from the hand of Holiness. Maybe the least eccentric thing I ever did in my life was for an hour or so on that long drive not just to glimpse that truth but to act on it. The trees waved their holy branches at my holiness. I waved my holy hand at theirs.

We live in a broken world, a world shattered by wars, famine, political upheaval. We are citizens of a nation that in all its history has perhaps never been so dramatically confronted as it is now by its brokenness—a nation whose streets are littered by the bodies of the homeless and where the gap between the rich and the poor widens every year, a nation that continues to spend billions on defense when what we need most to defend ourselves against are poverty, illiteracy, and the despair that breeds crime and addiction. As for the church of Christ, no one knows better than the church itself all the ways it too is broken, just as no one knows better than you and I the brokenness of our own lives. In other words it is easy enough to see the world as a horror show, but that is not the way the old crone in the dark little room saw it when she recognized beneath the darkness what she wrote of as the joy. For all its horrors, the world is not ultimately a horror show because, as Jesus tell us, the world has the Kingdom buried in it like a treasure buried in a field, like leaven working in dough, like a seed germinating in the earth, like whatever it was in the heart of the Prodigal Son that finally brought him home. The question is: how is it possible for us not just to glimpse that buried kingdom but to unbury and become it? How is it possible in a broken world to become whole? Is wholeness something that we reach by taking pains, taking thought? Is it something that is given to us by grace alone? Is wholeness a human possibility at all?

In *The Brothers Karamazov*, Dostoyevsky tries to answer that question in terms of a story, which is how one way or another we answer it—by living out the story of our own lives. Father Zossima, the holy Russian elder and monk, tells about something that happened to him once when he was a young officer in the czar's army. He had been in love with a young woman, and then, during a time when he was away for a few months, the young woman married another man. When Zossima came back and found out what had happened, he challenged the other man to a duel. Many years later, he describes the event like this.

> It was the end of June, and our meeting was to take place at seven o'clock the next day on the outskirts of town—and then something happened that in very truth was the turning-point of my life. In the evening, returning home in a savage and brutal humor, I flew into a rage with my orderly Afanasy, and gave him two blows in the face with all my might, so that it was covered with blood. He had not long been in my service and I had struck him before, but never with such ferocious cruelty. And, believe me, though it's forty years ago, I recall it now with shame and pain. I went to bed and slept for about three hours; when I waked up the day was breaking. I got up—I did not want to sleep any

more—I went to the window—opened it, it looked out upon the garden; I saw the sun rising; it was warm and beautiful, the birds were singing.

What's the meaning of it, I thought. I feel in my heart as it were something vile and shameful. Is it because I am going to shed blood? No, I thought, I feel it's not that. Can it be that I'm afraid of death, afraid of being killed? No, that's not it, that's not it at all. . . . And all at once I knew what it was; it was because I had beaten Afanasy the evening before. It all rose in my mind, it all was as it were repeated over again; he stood before me and I was beating him straight on the face and he was holding his arms stiffly down, his head erect, his eyes fixed upon me as though on parade. He staggered at every blow and did not even dare to raise his hands to protect himself. That is what a man has been brought to, and that was a man beating a fellow creature! What a crime! It was as though a sharp dagger had pierced me right through, I stood as if I were struck dumb, while the sun was shining, the leaves were rejoicing and the birds were trilling the praise of God. . . . I hid my face in my hands, fell on my bed and broke into a storm of tears. . . . Suddenly my second, the ensign, came in with the pistols to fetch me.

"Ah," said he, "it's a good thing you are up already, it's time we were off, come along!"

I did not know what to do and hurried to and fro undecided; we went out to the carriage however.

"Wait here a minute," I said to him. "I'll be back directly. I have forgotten my purse."

And I ran back alone, straight to Afanasy's little room.

"Afanasy," I said, "I gave you two blows on the face yesterday. Forgive me," I said.

He started as though he were frightened, and looked at me, and I saw that it was not enough, and on the spot, in my full officer's uniform, I dropped at his feet and bowed my head to the ground.

"Forgive me," I said.

Then he was completely aghast.

"Your honor. . . sir, what are you doing? Am I worth it?"

And he burst out crying as I had done before, hid his face in his hands, turned to the window and shook all over with his sobs. I flew out to my comrade and jumped into the carriage.

"Ready," I cried. "Have you ever seen a conqueror?" I asked him. "Here is one before you."

"Well, brother, you are a plucky fellow. You'll keep up the honour of the uniform, I can see."

So we reached the place and found them there, waiting for us. We were placed twelve paces apart; he had the first shot. I stood gaily, looking him full in the face; I did not twitch an eyelash. I looked lovingly at him, for I knew what I would do. His shot just grazed my cheek and ear.

"Thank God," I cried, "no man had been killed," and I seized my pistol, turned back and flung it far away into the wood.

"That's the place for you," I cried.

I turned to my adversary.

"Forgive me, young fool that I am, sir," I said, "for my unprovoked insult to you and for forcing you to fire at me. I am ten times worse than you and more, maybe. Tell that to the person whom you hold dearest in the world."

I had no sooner said this than they all three shouted at me.

"Upon my word," cried my adversary, annoyed, "if you did not want to fight why did you not let me alone?"

"Yesterday I was a fool, today I know better," I answered him gaily.

"As to yesterday, I believe you, but as for today, it is difficult to agree with your opinion," said he.

"Bravo," I cried, clapping my hands. "I agree with you there too. I have deserved it."

"Will you shoot, sir, or not?"

"No, I won't," I said. "If you like, fire at me again, but it would be better for you not to fire."

The seconds, especially mine, were shouting too: "Can you disgrace the regiment like this, facing your antagonist and begging his forgiveness! If I'd only known this!"

I stood facing them all, not laughing now.

"Gentlemen," I said, "is it really so wonderful in these days to find a man who can repent of his stupidity and publicly confess his wrongdoing?"

"But not in a duel," cried my second again.

"That's what's so strange," I said. "For I ought to have owned my fault as soon as I got here, before he had fired a shot, before leading him into a great and deadly sin; but we have made our life so grotesque, that to act in that way would have been almost impossible, for only after I had faced his shot at the distance of twelve paces could my words have any significance for him, and if I had spoken before, he would have said 'he is a coward, the sight of the pistols have frightened him, no use to listen to him.' Gentlemen," I cried suddenly, speaking straight from my heart, "look around you at the gifts of God, the clear sky, the pure air, the tender grass, the birds. Nature is beautiful and sinless, and we, only we, are sinful and foolish, and we don't understand that life is heaven, for we have only to understand that and it will at once be fulfilled in all its beauty. We shall embrace each other and weep."

I would have said more, but I could not; my voice broke with the sweetness and youthful gladness of it, and there was such bliss in my heart as I had never known before in my life.

Insofar as wholeness can be ours at all, is it ours by working for it or is it ours by grace? The answer, Dostoyevsky suggests, is that it is both, that wholeness involves the same mysterious partnership of the human and the divine that Saint Paul points to when he writes to the Ephesians, "By grace you have been saved, through faith" (Ephesians 2:8). The grace of it, the divine part of it, is the beautiful day that Zossima wakes up to—the sun rising and the birds singing not unlike the trees waving along the New York Thruway. The view from his window both blesses him with its beauty and at the same time, and no less graciously, opens his eyes to his own inner unbeauty, the agonizing shame he feels at having brutalized his orderly the night before. It is not so much that he is judged by the beauty he sees as that he is brought up short by it. The beauty he sees strips the scales from his eyes and calls him somehow to become beautiful himself. It is a call that rises out of the holiest part of who he is.

To *answer* that call is the human part of it, the part that Zossima himself must play. It is by no means a painless part. He begs Afanasy for forgiveness—an extraordinary act of self-abasement at any time, let alone among the rigid class distinctions of czarist Russia—and when Afanasy stands there stammering with disbelief, Zossima bows his head to the ground before him to make sure he understands. In the duel itself then, he refuses to fire a shot when his turn comes with the result that all the other officers, including the rival whose life he has spared, are aghast at such a breach of decorum and tell him that he has disgraced the regiment and must be either a fool or a madman.

The part he has to play, in other words, is not to kill his enemy but to kill everything that is broken and old in himself so that something whole and new can be born. Then as that newness starts coming to birth, he sees that the distinctions he has always made between enemies and friends, like the distinction between officers like him and peasants like Afanasy, are as absurd as everything he has always believed about honor and pride and the military code. "Nature is beautiful and sinless, and we, only we, are sinful and foolish, and we don't understand that life is heaven," he cries out. "We have only to understand that and it will at once be fulfilled in all its beauty, and we shall embrace one another and weep."

Zossima does not become a whole human being all in an instant, as the novel goes on to show. There is a long journey ahead of him still, as there is a long journey ahead of all of us still. But the grace of God, which reaches him through his vision of the beautiful day, opens not just his eyes to see that life is heaven but opens his heart where heaven has dwelled all along. The world thinks he has gone mad when he flings his pistol into the woods without firing a shot, but he finds himself filled with a peace that the catcalls of the world can no more take away than the applause of the world can give. He has a long way still to go, but he sets forth armed with the truth that only years later does he put into words. "Fathers and teachers, I ponder, 'What is hell?' I maintain that hell is the suffering of being unable to love." What Dostoyevsky tells us is that the journey toward wholeness for Zossima and for all of us is above all else a journey toward that capacity to love which is called compassion.

Zossima saying that we have only to see that life is heaven and we will all embrace one another and weep, and Naya writing with wit and grace, in a hand so shaky that she can barely hold her pen, about joy. The summer trees bowing and beckoning and reaching out to us as you and I, if we dare, reach out in turn to them. There is treasure buried in the field of every one of our days, even the bleakest or dullest, and it is our business, as we journey, to keep our eyes peeled for it.

"There lives the dearest freshness deep down things," Gerard Manley Hopkins wrote, "And though the last lights off the black West went / Oh, morning, at the brown brink eastward, springs— / Because the Holy Ghost over the bent / World broods with warm breast and with ah! bright wings" ("God's Grandeur"). It is our business, as we journey, to keep our hearts open to the bright-winged presence of the Holy Ghost within us and the Kingdom of God among us until little by little compassionate love begins to change from a moral exercise, from a matter of gritting our teeth and doing our good deed for the day, into a joyous, spontaneous, self-forgetting response to the most real aspect of all reality, which is that the world is holy because God made it and so is every one of us as well. To live as though that reality does not exist is to be a stranger in a world of strangers. To live out of and toward that reality is little by little to become whole.

Part 2

◆   ◆   ◆   ◆   ◆

THE HOME
WE DREAM

7

◇　◇　◇　◇　◇

The Great Dance

*After this Jesus revealed himself again to the disciples by the Sea of
Tiberias; and he revealed himself in this way. Simon Peter, Thomas
called the Twin, Nathanael of Cana in Galilee, the sons of Zebedee,
and two others of his disciples were together. Simon Peter said to them,
"I am going fishing." They said to him, "We will go with you." They
went out and got into the boat; but that night they caught nothing.*

*Just as day was breaking, Jesus stood on the beach; yet the disciples
did not know that it was Jesus. Jesus said to them, "Children, have you
any fish?" They answered him, "No." He said to them, "Cast the net on
the right side of the boat, and you will find some." So they cast it, and
now they were not able to haul it in, for the quantity of fish. That disci-
ple whom Jesus loved said to Peter, "It is the Lord!" When Simon Peter
heard that it was the Lord, he put on his clothes, for he was stripped for
work, and sprang into the sea. But the other disciples came in the boat,
dragging the net full of fish, for they were not far from the land, but
about a hundred yards off.*

*When they got out on land, they saw a charcoal fire there, with fish
lying on it, and bread. Jesus said to them, "Bring some of the fish that
you have just caught." So Simon Peter went aboard and hauled the net
ashore, full of large fish, a hundred and fifty-three of them; and al-
though there were so many, the net was not torn. Jesus said to them,
"Come and have breakfast." Now none of the disciples dared ask him,
"Who are you?" They knew it was the Lord. Jesus came and took the
bread and gave it to them and so with the fish.*

John 21:1–13

everal winters ago my wife and I and our then twenty-year-old daughter, Sharmy, went to that great tourist extravaganza near Orlando, Florida, called Sea World. There is a lot of hoopla to it—crowds of people, loud music, Mickey Mouse T-shirts, and so on, but the main attraction makes it all worthwhile. It takes place in a huge tank of crystal clear, turquoise water with a platform projecting out into it from the far side and on the platform several pretty young women and handsome young men in bathing suits who run things. It was a gorgeous day when we were there, with bright Florida sunlight reflected in the shimmering water and a cloudless blue sky over our heads. The bleachers where we sat were packed.

The way the show began was that at a given signal they released into the tank five or six killer whales, as we call them (it would be interesting to know what they call us), and no creatures under heaven could have looked less killerlike as they went racing around and around in circles. What with the dazzle of sky and sun, the beautiful young people on the platform, the soft southern air, and the crowds all around us watching the performance with a delight matched only by what seemed the delight of the performing whales, it was as if the whole creation—men and women and beasts and sun and water and earth and sky and, for all I know, God himself—was caught up in one great, jubilant dance of unimaginable beauty. And then, right in the midst of it, I was astonished to find that my eyes were filled with tears.

When the show was over and I turned to my wife and daughter beside me to tell them what had happened, their answer was to say that there had been tears also in their eyes. It wasn't until several years later that I happened to describe the incident at a seminar at the College of Preachers in Washington, and afterwards a man came up to me who turned out to be the dean of Salisbury Cathedral in England who asked me if I would take a look at part of a sermon he had preached a few weeks earlier. The passage he showed me was one that described how he had recently gone to a place near Orlando, Florida, called Sea World, and how he had seen an extraordinary spectacle there, in the midst of which he had suddenly discovered that his eyes were filled with tears.

My wife and I and our daughter Sharmy and the dean of Salisbury Cathedral—I believe there is no mystery about why we shed tears. We shed tears because we had caught a glimpse of the Peaceable Kingdom, and it had almost broken our hearts. For a few moments we had seen Eden and been part of the great dance that goes on at the heart of creation. We shed tears because we were given a glimpse of the way life was created to be and is not. We had seen why it was that "the morning stars sang together, and all the sons of God shouted for joy" when the world was first made, as the book of Job describes it, and of what it was that made Saint Paul write, even when he was in prison and on his way to execution, "Rejoice in the Lord always; again I will say, Rejoice." We had had a glimpse of part at least of what Jesus meant when he said, "Blessed are you that weep now, for you shall laugh."

The world is full of darkness, but what I think we caught sight of in that tourist trap in Orlando, Florida, of all places, was that at the heart of darkness—whoever would have believed it?—there is joy unimaginable. The world does bad things to us all, and we do bad things to the world and to each other and maybe most of all to ourselves, but in that dazzle of bright water as the glittering whales hurled themselves into the sun, I believe what we saw was that joy is what we belong to. Joy is home, and I believe the tears that came to our eyes were more than anything else homesick tears. God created us in joy and created us for joy, and in the long run not all the darkness there is in the world and in ourselves can separate us finally from that joy, because whatever else it means to say that God created us in his image, I think it means that even when we cannot believe in him, even when we feel most spiritually bankrupt and deserted by him, his mark is deep within us. We have God's joy in our blood.

I believe that joy is what our tears were all about and what our faith is all about too. Not happiness. Happiness comes when things are going our way, which makes it only a forerunner to the unhappiness that inevitably follows when things stop going our way, as in the end they will stop for all of us. Joy, on the other hand, does not come because something is happening or not happening but every once in a while rises up out of simply being alive, of being part of the terror as well as the fathomless richness of the world that God has made. When Jesus was eating his last meal with his friends, knowing that his death was only a few hours away, he was in no sense happy, nor did he offer his friends happiness any more than he offers happiness to you and me. What he offers is more precious than happiness because it is beyond the world's power either to give or take away. "These things have I spoken to you," he said, "that my joy may be in you"—joy, as poignant as grief, that brings tears to the eyes as it did to mine that afternoon in the crowded bleachers.

Could anyone guess by looking at us that joy is at the heart of what goes on in church Sunday after Sunday? Are we given any glimpses there of what it was that blazed forth with such power in Orlando? I hope so. I pray so. Maybe in the freshness and fragrance of the flowers on the altar we catch some flicker of it, and in the candles' burning. Maybe we can feel some reverberation of it in just all of us being together as human beings longing for and reaching out for we are not quite sure what. Maybe every once in a great while something joyful stirs in us as the taste of wine touches our tongues or some phrase of a hymn or prayer or sermon comes alive for a second and touches our hearts. The crimson and peacock blue of a stained glass window with the sun shining through it can sometimes speak of it the way jewels do. But in all honesty I have to confess that I for one have found little joy like that in the churches we go to year after year, very little of what made the great whales leap into the sky.

We are above all things loved—that is the good news of the gospel—and loved not just the way we turn up on Sundays in our best clothes and on our best behavior and with our best feet forward, but loved as we alone know ourselves to be, the weakest and shabbiest of who we are along with the strongest and gladdest. To come together as people who believe that just maybe this gospel is actually true should be to come together like people who have just won the Irish Sweepstakes. It should have us throwing our arms around each other like people who have just discovered that every single man and woman in those pews is not just another familiar or unfamiliar face but is our long-lost brother and our long-lost sister because despite the fact that we have all walked in different gardens and knelt at different graves, we have all, humanly speaking, come from the same place and are heading out into the same blessed mystery that awaits us all. This is the joy that is so apt to be missing, and missing not just from church but from our own lives—the joy of not just managing to believe at least part of the time that it is true that life is holy but of actually running into that holiness head-on the way my wife and my daughter and the English dean and I each ran into it in the splendor of that moment we shared. I think maybe it is holiness that we long for more than we long for anything else.

In the last chapter of John's Gospel there is another moment that has certain features in common with the moment at Sea World. It, also, has water in it and fish in it, and the sun, and the sky, and, unless I miss my guess, tears in the eyes of at least some of the ones who were there when it happened. The water was the Sea of Tiberias, where the fishermen disciples carried on their trade. The crucifixion had taken place over a week earlier. Jesus had appeared to some of them since then and had said things and promised things—Thomas had even touched his hand—but then again he was gone.

One night Peter rounded up six of his friends, and together they went out fishing. They failed to catch anything, but maybe it was less fish they were after than just a way of getting through another night without the one they had lost. Then "just as day was breaking, " John says, about a hundred yards away on the beach, they saw the glow of a charcoal fire and a man standing by it whom at first they didn't recognize. The man asked them if they had had any luck, and when they said they had not, he told them to try throwing their nets off the starboard side, and this time they were lucky to the tune of what John says were a hundred and fifty-three fish, as if he had actually counted them at the time and never forgotten the number. Then one of the disciples saw that the man on the beach was Jesus, and when he told Peter, Peter hurled himself into the water like a whale and somehow swam and scrambled his way to shore ahead of everybody else.

The brief conversation he had with Jesus is a haunting one, because what Peter says is so close to what I suspect you and I would have said if we had been there ourselves, and because what Jesus says to Peter is so close to what he says to all of us. Jesus asks Peter if he loves him, and Peter says yes, he does. He says he loves him. Even when you have never seen Jesus, as you and I have never seen him, it is hard not to love him, at least a little. Even when you are not sure who Jesus is or what you are supposed to believe about him—even when you have never been very good, God knows, at following him, whatever that means—even then, I think, you can't help loving him in at least some half-embarrassed, half-hidden way. Three times Jesus makes Peter say he loves him, and each time Jesus answers him virtually the same way. "Feed my lambs," he says. "Tend my sheep," he says. "Feed my sheep."

I think the kind of joy that brings tears to our eyes has much to do with what Jesus means by feeding each other. There are people who are literally starving for want of food, and there are other people, closer to home, who may be starving for want of nothing so much as whatever we ourselves can give them in the way of God only knows what small but life-restoring act of kindness and understanding. Literally or figuratively, for you and me to feed each other, to tend to each other's needs, one way or another to take care of each other is more and more to become part of that dance of earth and sky and men and women and water and beasts that according to the Psalmist makes the floods clap their hands and the hills sing together for joy.

"Feed my sheep," Jesus said to Peter as the first rays of the sun went fanning out across the sky, but, before that, he said something else. The six other men had beached the boat by then and had come up to the charcoal fire knowing that it was Jesus who was standing there and yet not quite knowing, not quite brave enough to ask him if he was the one they were all but certain he was. He told them to bring him some of the fish they had just hauled in, and then he said something that, if I had to guess, was what brought tears to their eyes if anything did. The Lamb of God. The Prince of Peace. The Dayspring from on High. Instead of all the extraordinary words we might imagine on his lips, what he said was, "Come and have breakfast."

I believe he says it to all of us: to feed his sheep, his lambs, to be sure, but first to let him feed us—to let him feed us with something of himself. In the sip of wine and crumb of bread. In the dance of sun and water and sky. In the faces of the people who need us most and of the people we most need. In the smell of breakfast cooking on a charcoal fire. Who knows where we will find him or whether we will recognize him if we do? Who knows anything even approaching the truth of who he really was? But my prayer is that we will all of us find him somewhere, somehow, and that he will give us something of his life to fill our emptiness, something of his light to drive back our dark.

8

◇ ◇ ◇ ◇ ◇

The News of the Day

Woe to you that are rich, for you have received your consolation.
Woe to you that are full now, for you shall hunger.
Woe to you that laugh now, for you shall mourn and weep.

Luke 6:24–25

It gets to be six-thirty or seven in the evening, say, and we switch the TV on to Peter Jennings or Tom Brokaw or MacNeil and Lehrer if we are really serious about it and then settle back and listen as they tell us the news of the day. It is a way of keeping in touch with reality, of maintaining perspective, of taking stock. It is a way of reminding ourselves that beyond the little world we live in, there is another, wider world that we are all part of although we get so caught up in the business of our own worlds that we tend to forget about it.

Every evening the news is different, of course, and yet there seem to be certain major themes that keep on recurring day after

day and year after year. There are always wars going on some-
where. In the Middle East, in Africa, in our own streets, there are
always people fighting other people for control, for power, for re-
venge, for freedom, for a bigger slice of the pie.

On the other side of the coin, the news of the day always in-
volves also the search for peace. Heads of state get together to air
old grievances and consider new possibilities of accommodation
and compromise. The Arab sits down with the Jew. Labor sits down
with management. Just as much as the world is always fighting, the
world is also always searching for a way to bring the fighting to an
end and to have peace.

And the world is always hungry. Hunger is another of the great
recurring themes. The statistics are so appalling that we cannot
keep them in our heads or choose not to. Not just in the Third
World, but all over the world people are starving to death, hun-
dreds of thousands of them, and thousands of them children. In
Manchester, Vermont, near where I live, a crowd of people line up
at the senior center on School Street every week to pick up enough
of the food collected by the local churches to keep the wolf from
their doors because even in this country, surrounded by affluence,
there are countless families that can afford either a home to live in
or food to eat but not both.

And that leads to the last of the recurring themes, which is
homelessness. When I was a child in New York, if you wanted to
see people sleeping on the streets, you had go down to places like
the Bowery to see them. Nowadays there are people sleeping in all
the streets—not just the slum streets but the fancy streets too, and
not just in New York, God knows, but in cities all over this country.
They lie on the sidewalks, on hot-air gratings, in station waiting

rooms till somebody kicks them out, in doorways, and on the steps of churches. Even on the coldest winter nights you see them there in their cardboard boxes and filthy clothes padded out with old newspaper for extra warmth. They are the dispossessed and forgotten ones. They are the ones without shelter, without any place that belongs to them or where they belong. As someone once put it, home is the place where, if you have to go there, they have to take you in, and these people have no such place anywhere in the world.

The fighting. The search for peace. Hunger. Homelessness. Every evening we sit in our living rooms and watch on the flickering screen what has gone on in the world that day. What we choose to do about it, you and I—what worthy causes, if any, get our time and energy, what political candidates get our votes, how much money we give away or could afford to give away if our hearts were really in it—those are all issues of the greatest and most far-reaching importance not just for the saving of the world but for the saving of our own souls. But without leaving those issues behind, we would do well to focus also on another kind of news of the day—another kind of taking stock, another kind of reality to keep in touch with.

Beyond what goes on in the world that makes the headlines, there is also what goes on in the small, private worlds that you and I move around in and the news of our own individual days in those worlds. Some of the things that happen in them are so small that we hardly notice them, and some of them shake the very ground beneath our feet, but, whether they are great or small, they make up the day-by-day story of who we are and of what we are doing with our lives and what our lives are doing to us. Their news is the news of what we are becoming or failing to become.

Maybe the best time to look at that news is at night when we first turn out the light and are lying in the dark waiting for sleep to come. It is a time to look back at the wars that you and I have been engaged in for the last twenty-four hours, or twenty-four years for that matter, because there are none of us who do not one way or another wage war every day if only with ourselves. It is a time to look back at our own searches for peace because deep beneath the level of all the other things we spend our time searching for, peace, real peace, is the treasure for which maybe we would all of us be willing to trade every other treasure we have. As we lie there in the dark, we might ask ourselves, what battles, if any, are we winning? What battles are we losing? Which battles might we do better not to be fighting at all, and which, in place of surrender, should we be fighting more effectively and bravely ? We are church-goers. We are nice people. We fight well camouflaged. We are snipers rather than bombardiers. Our weapons are more apt to be chilly silences than hot words. But our wars are no less real for all of that, and the stakes are no less high.

Perhaps the stakes are nowhere higher than in the war we all wage within ourselves—the battles we fight against loneliness, boredom, despair, self-doubt, the battles against fear, against the great dark. In the whole Bible there are perhaps no words that everybody, everywhere, can identify with more fully than the ones Saint Paul wrote to the Roman church: "I do not do the good I want, but the evil I do not want is what I do" (7:19). That is as rich a summation as any I know of the inner battle that we are all involved in, which is the battle to break free from all the camouflaged and not so camouflaged hostilities that we half deplore even as we engage in them, the battle to become what we have it in us at our best to be, which is wise and loving friends both to our own selves and to each other as we reach out not only for what we need to have but also for what we need to give.

These are the wars that go on within families, within marriages, the wars we wage with each other sometimes openly but more often so hiddenly that even in the thick of them we are hardly aware of what we are doing. These are the wars that go on between parents and children, between people who at one level are friends but at another level are adversaries, competitors, strangers even, with a terrible capacity for wounding each other and being wounded by each other no less deeply and painfully because the wounds are invisible and the bleeding mostly internal. Sometimes we fight to survive, sometimes just to be noticed, let alone to be loved. Sniping and skirmishing, defensive maneuvers, naked aggressions, and guerrilla subversions are part of the lives of all of us.

In Ken Burns's television series on the Civil War, the narrator describes a remarkable scene that took place on the fiftieth anniversary of the Battle of Gettysburg in 1913, when what was left of the two armies decided to stage a reenactment of Pickett's charge. All the old Union veterans up on the ridge took their places among the rocks, and all the old Confederate veterans started marching toward them across the field below, and then the extraordinary thing happened. As the old men among the rocks began to rush down at the old men coming across the field, a great cry went up, only instead of doing battle as they had half a century earlier, this time they threw their arms around each other. They embraced each other and openly wept.

As we lie in the dark looking back over the news of one more day of our lives coming to an end, we might ask ourselves which of the obscure little wars we all engage in could end that same way if only we had eyes to see what those old men saw as they fell into each other's arms on the field of Gettysburg. If only we could see that the people we are one way or another at war with are, more often than not, less to blame for the bad blood between us than we are, because, again more often than not, the very faults we find so unbearable in them are apt to be versions of the same faults that we are more or less blind to in ourselves.

One evening at dinner not long ago I found myself sitting next to a woman I have known for years. She is someone I have valued and admired in all sorts of ways, but for one reason or another, as much because of me as because of her, the air between us was often shadowed and bent. I found myself telling her a dream I had had about her a few nights before. I told her I had dreamed that I was sitting beside her, much as I was sitting beside her there at the dinner table telling her about it, and that suddenly I had turned to her and said, "I love you." I then told her something else which I don't think I fully realized until that moment. I told her that what I had said to her in the dream was true. I saw immediately that she was as moved as I was, and all at once the air between us was no longer bent but was full of healing and kindness. It was only a very small moment, but in terms of the news of that day of my life, it marked the end of a war and gave me at least a glimpse of the peace that she and I and all of us hunger above all else to find.

Hunger in the literal sense is unknown to you and me. In a world where thousands starve to death every day, we live surrounded by plenty. With full bellies we watch the TV footage of Third World children with their bellies swollen, their legs and arms like sticks, eyes vacant in their ancient faces, and may God have mercy on us as a nation, as a civilization, as whatever it means to call us Christendom, if we do not find some way to wipe their hunger from the face of the earth. And may God have mercy upon us too if we fail to recognize that even in the midst of plenty, we have our own terrible hungers.

We hunger to be known and understood. We hunger to be loved. We hunger to be at peace inside our own skins. We hunger not just to be fed these things but, often without realizing it, we hunger to feed others these things because they too are starving for them. We hunger not just to be loved but to love, not just to be forgiven but to forgive, not just to be known and understood for all the good times and bad times that for better or worse have made us who we are, but to know and understand each other to the point of seeing that, in the last analysis, we all have the same good times, the same bad times, and that for that very reason there is no such thing in all the world as anyone who is really a stranger.

When Jesus commanded us to love our neighbors as ourselves, it was not just for our neighbors' sakes that he commanded it, but for our own sakes as well. Not to help find some way to feed the children who are starving to death is to have some precious part of who we are starve to death with them. Not to give of ourselves to the human beings we know who may be starving not for food but for what we have in our hearts to nourish them with is to be, ourselves, diminished and crippled as human beings.

We lie in our beds in the dark. There is a picture of the children on the bureau. Our clothes hang in the closet. There is a patch of moonlight on the carpeted floor. We live surrounded by the comfort of familiar things, sights, sounds. When the weather is bad, we have shelter. When things are bad in our lives, we have a place where we can retreat to lick our wounds and pull ourselves back together again, while tens of thousands of people, thousands of them children, wander the streets looking for some doorway to lie down in out of the wind. "Woe to you that are rich," Jesus said, "for you have received your consolation. Woe to you that are full now, for you shall hunger. Woe to you that laugh now, for you shall mourn and weep." It is a text that is not often preached on to people like us because it cuts too close to the bone, but woe to us indeed if we forget the homeless ones who have no vote, no power, nobody to lobby for them, and who might as well have no faces even, the way we try to avoid the troubling sight of them in the streets of the cities where they roam like stray cats. And as we listen each night to the news of what happened in our lives that day, woe to us too if we forget our own homelessness.

To be homeless the way people like you and me are apt to be homeless is to have homes all over the place but not to be really at home in any of them. To be really at home is to be really at peace, and our lives are so intricately interwoven that there can be no real peace for any of us until there is real peace for all of us. That is the truth that underlies not just the news of the world but the news of every one of our own days.

9

◊   ◊   ◊   ◊   ◊

The Secret in the Dark

That very day two of them were going to a village named Emmaus, about seven miles from Jerusalem, and talking with each other about all these things that had happened. While they were talking and discussing together, Jesus himself drew near and went with them. But their eyes were kept from recognizing him. And he said to them, "What is this conversation which you are holding with each other as you walk?" And they stood still, looking sad. Then one of them, named Cleopas, answered him, "Are you the only visitor to Jerusalem who does not know the things that have happened there in these days?" And he said to them, "What things?" And they said to him, "Concerning Jesus of Nazareth, who was a prophet mighty in deed and word before God and all the people, and how our chief priests and rulers delivered him up to be condemned to death, and crucified him. But we had hoped that he was the one to redeem Israel. Yes, and besides all this, it is now the third day since this happened. Moreover, some women of our company amazed us. They were at the tomb early in the morning and did not find his body; and they came back saying that they had even seen a vision of angels, who said that he was alive. Some of those who were with us went to the tomb, and found it just as the woman had said; but him they did not see." And he said to them, "O foolish men, and slow of heart to believe all that the prophets have spoken! Was it not necessary that the Christ should suffer these things and enter into his glory?" And beginning with Moses and all the prophets, he interpreted to them in all the scriptures the things concerning himself.

*So they drew near to the village to which they were going. He appeared
to be going further, but they constrained him, saying, "Stay with us, for
it is toward evening and the day is now far spent." So he went in to stay
with them. When he was at table with them, he took the bread and
blessed, and broke it, and gave it to them. And their eyes were opened
and they recognized him; and he vanished out of their sight.*

Luke 24:13–31

I t has always struck me as remarkable that when the writers of
the four Gospels come to the most important part of the story
they have to tell, they tell it in whispers. The part I mean, of
course, is the part about the resurrection. The Jesus who was dead
is not dead anymore. He has risen. He is here. According to the
Gospels there was no choir of angels to proclaim it. There was no
sudden explosion of light in the sky. Not a single soul was around
to see it happen. When Mary Magdalen arrived at the tomb after-
ward, she thought at first that it must be a gardener standing there
in the shadows, and when she saw who it really was and tried to
embrace him, he told her not to, as if for fear that once she had
him in her arms she would never let him go, the way I suspect that
if you and I were ever to have him in our arms, we would never let
him go either. When the disciples heard he was alive again, they
tended to dismiss it as too good to be true, and even when they fi-
nally saw him for themselves, Thomas still wasn't convinced until
Jesus let him touch his wounds with his own hands. Later on,
when they were out fishing at daybreak, they saw him standing on
the beach, and there again they failed to recognize him until he

asked them to come join him at the charcoal fire he had started on the sand and cooked them breakfast.

The way the Gospel writers tell it, in other words, Jesus came back from death not in a blaze of glory but more like a candle flame in the dark, flickering first in this place, then in that place, then in no place at all. If they had been making the whole thing up for the purpose of converting the world, presumably they would have described it more the way the book of Revelation describes how he will come back again at the end of time with "the armies of heaven arrayed in fine linen, white and pure," as Revelation puts it, and his eyes "like a flame of fire, and on his head many diadems" (19:14, 12). But that is not the way the Gospels tell it. They are not trying to describe it as convincingly as they can. They are trying to describe it as truthfully as they can. It was the most extraordinary thing they believed had ever happened, and yet they tell it so quietly that you have to lean close to be sure what they are telling. They tell it as softly as a secret, as something so precious, and holy, and fragile, and unbelievable, and true, that to tell it any other way would be somehow to dishonor it. To proclaim the resurrection the way they do, you would have to say it in whispers: "Christ has risen." Like that.

Down through the centuries the Christian church, needless to say, has not whispered it but shouted it, and who can blame it? It was Saint Paul who was blunt enough to come straight out and write to the Corinthians, "If Christ has not been raised [from the dead], then our preaching is in vain and your faith is in vain" (1 Corinthians 15:14). So when churches all over the world proclaim that he has been raised indeed and our faith gloriously vindicated, they naturally do so at the top of their lungs and with all flags flying.

Banks of lilies on the altar. A full choir singing Bach or Handel. A resounding sermon. Fancy clothes. Packed pews. It can be a very powerful and beautiful occasion proclaiming that even in a mad and murderous world like ours, which no longer believes in much of anything, there are still people who believe that this miracle of all miracles actually took place, or who at least long to believe it, at least believe that it is of all miracles the one that would be most wonderful to be able to believe if only they could. But the shadow side of the great Easter celebration is that sometimes the very fanfare and fortissimo of it are apt to leave us feeling like the only guests at a great New Year's Eve party who are not having the time of our lives. All the wonderful things that are going on around us on Easter Sunday can sometimes make us more conscious than usual that nothing even close to all that wonderful is going on inside ourselves.

That is why the Sundays after Easter are so precious, and precious because, in their comparatively subdued, low-key way, they seem not only closer to how the resurrection actually took place as the Gospels describe it but, more important still, closer to the reality of the resurrection as you and I are apt to experience it. These everyday Sundays without all the flowers and music and exaltation are like the kind of day that Luke describes in his account of the two disciples on their walk from Jerusalem to Emmaus some seven miles away.

They had heard the women's report about finding the tomb of Jesus empty that morning, but as Luke writes, it "seemed to them an idle tale, and they did not believe them." They did not believe the women because they found what the women said unbelievable, and then as they trudged along with the evening approaching and the sun starting to set, Jesus himself—risen from the dead and alive again—joined them on their way only they did not know it was Jesus because, again as Luke puts it, "their eyes were kept from recognizing him," and I think those eyes are almost the most haunting part of the whole haunting story because they remind me so much of my own eyes and because I suspect they may remind you also of yours. How extraordinary to have eyes like that— eyes that look out at this world we live in but, more often than not, see everything except what matters most.

In Florida, in the winter, there is a walk that I take early in the morning before breakfast most days. It doesn't go to Emmaus exactly, unless maybe that's exactly where it does go, but in the literal sense it takes me some three miles or so along a completely uninhabited stretch of the inland waterway that separates the barrier island where we live from the mainland. I do not know any place lovelier on the face of this planet, especially at that early hour when there is nobody else around and everything is so fresh and still. The waterway drifts by like a broad river. The ponds reflect the sky. There are wonderful birds—snow-white egrets and ibis, boat-tail grackles black as soot—and long, unbroken vistas of green grass and trees. It is a sight worth traveling a thousand miles to see, and yet there is no telling how hard I have to struggle, right there in the midst of it, actually to see it.

What I do instead is think about things I have been doing and things I have to do. I think about people I love and people I do not know how to love. I think about letters to write and things around the house to get fixed and old grievances and longings and regrets. I worry and dream about the future. That is to say, I get so lost in my own thoughts—and *lost* is just the word for it, as lost as you can get in a strange town where you don't know the way—that I have to struggle to see where I am, almost to *be* where I am. Much of the time I might as well be walking in the dark or sitting at home with my eyes closed, those eyes that keep me from recognizing what is happening around me.

But then every once in a while, by grace, I recognize at least some part of it. Every once in a while I recognize that I am walking in green pastures that call out to me to lie down in them, and beside still waters where my feet lead me. Sometimes in the way the breeze stirs the palms or the way a bird circles over my head, I recognize that even in the valley of the shadow of my own tangled thoughts there is something holy and unutterable seeking to restore my soul. I see a young man in a checked shirt riding a power mower, and when I wave my hand at him, he waves his hand at me and I am hallowed by his greeting. I see a flock of white birds rising, and my heart rises with them.

And then there is one particular tree, a tree that I always see because it is the northernmost one I come to and marks the spot where I turn around and start for home. The label on it says that it is a Cuban laurel, but its true and secret name has nothing to do with labels. It has multiple trunks all braided and buttressed, and roots that snake out over the ground as widely as its branches snake out into the air. Here and there from one of the larger branches it has sent down a slender air-root, which in time turns into another trunk that supports its weight like a sinewy old arm. There are one or two places where the leaves have gone brown and brittle, but the tree holds them high into the sky as proudly and gallantly as it holds the green ones. At the risk of being spotted as a hopeless eccentric, I always stop for a moment and touch the coarse-grained, gray bark of it with my hand, or sometimes with my cheek, which I suppose is a way of blessing it for being so strong and so beautiful. Who knows how many years it has been standing there in fair weather and foul, sending down all those extra trunks to keep itself from breaking apart and wearing its foliage like a royal crown even though part of it is dying? And I think it is because of that quality of sheer endurance that on one particular morning I found myself touching it not to bless it for once, but to ask its blessing, so that I myself might move toward old age and death with something like its stunning grace and courage.

"When I was hungry, you gave me food, when I was naked you clothed me," Jesus said. "When I was a stranger, you welcomed me." And "When I was a tree," he might have said, "you blessed me and asked my blessing." To believe that Christ is risen and alive in the world is to believe that there is no place or person or thing in the world through which we ourselves may not be made more alive by his life, and whenever we *are* made more alive, whenever we are made more brave and strong and beautiful, we may be sure that Christ is present with us even though more often than not our eyes, like the two disciples' eyes, are kept from recognizing him.

What kept them from recognizing him, of course, was that they thought he was dead and gone, and when he asked them what they had been talking about, that is what they told him in words as full of pathos as any in the New Testament. "We had hoped that he was the one to redeem Israel," they said, but by then their hope was as dead as they believed he was himself. They had gone to the tomb to see if he was alive as some believed but had found no trace of him. Like me on my walk, they were so lost in their sad and tangled thoughts that they did not recognize him any more than you and I would probably recognize him as we walk through the world because, like theirs, our eyes are too accustomed to darkness and our faith not strong enough to believe in the reality of light even if it were to blaze up before us.

Schindler's List is a movie about the Holocaust. It is a movie about Oskar Schindler, who was a wartime profiteer, a womanizer, a boozer, a good friend of the Nazis, yet who for reasons even he apparently didn't understand became obsessed with the idea of saving as many Jews as he could from the gas ovens of Auschwitz by commandeering them to work in one of his factories and ended up saving some eleven hundred of them. It is about Oskar Schindler, the Nazi saint. It is about a dark and anguished world where again and again in the faces of the persecuted Jews as they appear on the screen you see the face of Christ while their persecutors saw only a people to be wiped from the face of the earth. It is about an inhuman, ex-human young commandant of a Nazi death camp who has the face of a fallen angel, the face of someone in whom the Christ who dwells in all of us is as dead as the Christ who dwells in all of us can ever be. And it is also about a little girl in a red dress.

The movie is filmed almost entirely in black and white like a documentary or an old newsreel, but every once in a while, usually in some crowd scene of children playing or people running or being herded into freight cars, you see, flickering like a candle flame in the seething grayness, one single touch of color in the form of a little girl dressed in red. You see her in her red dress hiding herself under a bed while the Nazis set about systematically shooting all the Jews they can lay their hands on in the Krakow ghetto, and then again here, then there, until finally for the last time you see a patch of the same red dress buried almost out of sight in a mountain of the dead left when the massacre has been completed.

I believe that although the two disciples did not recognize Jesus on the road to Emmaus, Jesus recognized them, that he saw them as if they were the only two people in the world. And I believe that the reason why the resurrection is more than just an extraordinary event which took place some two thousand years ago and then was over and done with is that, even as I speak these words and you listen to them, he also sees each of us like that. In this dark world where you and I see so little because of our unrecognizing eyes, he, whose eye is on the sparrow, sees each one of us as the child in red. And I believe that because he sees us, not even in the darkness of death are we lost to him or lost to each other. I believe that whether we recognize him or not, or believe in him or not, or even know his name, again and again he comes and walks a little way with us along whatever road we're following. And I believe that through something that happens to us, or something we see, or somebody we know—who can ever guess how or when or where?—he offers us, the way he did at Emmaus, the bread of life, offers us a new hope, a new vision of light that not even the dark world can overcome.

That is the word that on Easter Sunday is sounded forth on silver trumpets. And when Easter is past and the silver trumpets have faded away to hardly more than a distant echo, that is the word that is whispered to us like a secret in the dark, the saving and holy word that flickers among us like a red dress in a gray world.

10

◇ ◇ ◇ ◇ ◇

Two Narrow Words

Then Job answered:
"Today also my complaint is bitter;
    his hand is heavy despite my groaning.
Oh, that I knew where I might find him,
    that I might come even to his dwelling!
I would lay my case before him,
    and fill my mouth with arguments. . . .
If I go forward, he is not there;
    or backward, I cannot perceive him;
on the left he hides, and I cannot behold him;
    I turn to the right, but I cannot see him. . . .
If only I could vanish in darkness,
    and thick darkness would cover my face."

    Job 23:1–17 passim, NRSV

We do not want you to be unaware, brothers and sisters, of the afflic-
tion we experienced in Asia; for we were so utterly, unbearably crushed
that we despaired of life itself. Indeed, we felt that we had received the
sentence of death so that we would not rely on ourselves but on God
who raises the dead. He who rescued us from so deadly a peril will con-
tinue to rescue us; on him we have set our hope that he will rescue us
again. . . .

    2 Corinthians 1:8–10, NRSV

O eloquent, just and mightie Death! Whom none could advise, thou hast persuaded; what none hath dared, thou hast done; and whom all the world hath flattered, thou only hast cast out of the world and despised. Thou hast drawn together all the far-stretched greatness, all the pride, cruelty, and ambition of man, and covered it all over with these two narrow words: *hic jacet.*

Sir Walter Raleigh

So wrote the brilliant and ill-starred Sir Walter Raleigh at the end of his *History of the World,* and you cannot enter the ancient building of Westminster Abbey, I think, without some echo of his words sounding deep within you and making you catch your breath. *Hic jacet.* "Here lies." And there they all lie indeed, including Edward the Confessor, who was a holy saint, and many of his successors who were holy terrors; and both twelve-year-old Edward V and, not far away, his uncle Richard of Gloucester, who, if he didn't actually have him murdered as Tudor historians contend, at least had him declared a bastard and usurped his throne. Charles Dickens lies there too, the champion of the poor and dispossessed, and in un-marked graves beneath visitors' feet who knows how many of the poor and dispossessed themselves.

If their ghosts were to arise and stand there in the Abbey now, nowhere in Christendom would there be a richer assemblage of great ones and obscure ones, wise ones and foolish ones, proud ones and humble ones, saints and scoundrels; and in our own way you and I are just such a rich and miscellaneous assemblage within our single selves.

We are wise, and we are also foolish. In some ways we are rich and powerful and in other ways poor and helpless. To some we are friends but to others, or even to the same ones, we are enemies, enemies sometimes even to ourselves. There are days when our faith in God is strong and sustaining, and there are days when it is hard to believe that God exists at all. It is this inner complexity we share that makes each one of us a kind of walking Westminster Abbey and that unites us not only with each other but also with the fabled ghosts who haunt its shadows. And we are united with them too in that we, like them, will one day be covered by those same two narrow words.

There they lie, and if not in the Abbey, the chances are, then most surely somewhere else, we too will someday lie because just as they all came to face at last that eloquent, just, and mightie foe, so we also will come to face him, and in the meantime—although we have much to rejoice in and much to hold fast to and many days, we hope, still left ahead of us to live—we must somehow come to terms with the darkness not just of death but also of life. And that is of course the darkness that our two texts speak to and confront us with.

Where can we look for hope then? To what, to whom, can we turn when the shadows gather around us and within us? These are the questions that Job asks and that Saint Paul asks. They are the questions that Richard of Gloucester must have asked, no less than the two little princes in the Tower. It is the question that we all of us must ask and go on asking. "Whom none could advise, thou hast persuaded; what none hath dared, thou hast done." Is there anything in our faith to strengthen us against such an adversary as that—not just against death but against the whole deadly side of things like suffering and sorrow and loss and growing old that fore-shadow death's coming?

Everybody knows Job's story. He was "a blameless and upright man who feared God and turned away from evil," we are told, and he was also a very rich man with great quantities of cattle and land and servants and children to carry on his name. Then came the famous wager in which Satan, the adversary, bet God that if Job were ever to fall on evil times, his faith would be destroyed and, instead of worshiping God, he would curse him to his face. God accepted the wager and little by little allowed Satan to make terrible things happen to this blameless and upright man. His cattle died, his servants were put to the sword, his children were all killed, so that in the end he had nothing left to sustain him except for his all but devastated faith in a God who his whole life long he had thought rewarded the righteous with prosperity and visited only the wicked with horrors such as had befallen him. If God was just, how could he permit such unspeakable injustice? That was the question he addressed to God, and in the meanwhile how could he even get God to listen to him, to hear his case? It is an ancient folk tale that goes back a thousand years or more before the author of the book of Job used it as the basis for his great poem, but it has survived all these tens of centuries because of course the question itself has survived to become also our question. If God is all he's cracked up to be, then for God's sake, for Christ's sweet sake, where is he?

It is God alone who can answer the question, but where is God when our need for him is most desperate? "Behold, I go forward, but he is not there; and backward, but I cannot perceive him," Job cries out. "On the left hand I seek him, but I cannot behold him; I turn to the right hand, but I cannot see him." Is there anyone who at one dark time or another has not echoed Job's cry from the depths—a cry to the Creator to enter the creation and make all things right? But is such a thing possible even to God? In what conceivable way could God, as God, enter the world he has made in love without destroying it with his overwhelming presence?

By way of analogy, I think of William Shakespeare as creator and god of the plays he wrote trying to make himself known somehow to Cymbeline, say, or to Juliet, whose only reality is the plays that contain them and who know no more of true reality than they know what a midsummer night is truly, or a tempest, because all they have to go by is what Shakespeare scratched down about them with a quill. I think of the great playwright shouting out the devastating truth about who he is and about who they are to Lady Macbeth, for instance, who can hear only the raven croaking himself hoarse at the fatal entrance of Duncan under her battlements, or to Hamlet, who has ears only for his father's ghost. I think of him pounding his Elizabethan fist down on the crabbed manuscript before him to make himself heard and not a single one of them so much as turning a hair.

The characters in the world of Shakespeare's plays cannot hear Shakespeare or see him or know him directly any more than we can know God in God's world directly because even though there is nothing in the world of the plays, including themselves, that does not draw its only life from his life, his ways are not their ways, and whereas Shakespeare dwells in what amounts to eternity by contrast with anything they can imagine, they dwell only in the five acts' worth of make-believe time allotted to them on the printed page.

So how else could Shakespeare reach them then? If he were able somehow actually to enter the world of the plays as himself in all his multidimensional richness and fullness, if he were able somehow to thrust himself bodily into their fictive and derivative world, leap down feet foremost into their midst with a terrible ripping and scattering of parchment, how could it do anything less than blow the whole show sky-high?

Maybe the best he could manage would be to write himself into the plays as yet another character, into the fourth act of *King Lear*, for instance, where the Duke of Gloucester, betrayed by his bastard and blinded by his enemies, cries out, "As flies to wanton boys are we to the gods. They kill us for their sport." Let us say that Shakespeare, hearing Gloucester's anguish, appears at his side in the role of a shepherd, perhaps, or some homeless wanderer, takes him by the arm and tells him that his suffering is not the work of wanton gods at all but a precious and holy suffering which, before it kills him, will confer on him a strength and self-knowledge he would never have attained in any other way, one that will add to the depth and beauty of the whole world he inhabits as well as to his own depth and beauty. Would Gloucester believe him? Would he find comfort and healing in his words? Would he recognize him as the great Author himself, incarnate in the little world of the drama whose author he is? My guess is that he would not. My guess is that he would take him only for another half-crazed Tom O'Bedlam in a world gone mad.

Suppose then that Shakespeare went further still and decided to take Gloucester's suffering from him altogether. Suppose he reworked the entire play so that Edmund would never betray him and Cornwall and Regan never put out his eyes. Could he do such a thing without not only destroying the whole magnificent drama as he conceived it but also in a sense destroying Gloucester himself by so high-handedly altering his destiny? Part of an author's genius, which one might say is also part of God's genius, is never to manipulate his people like puppets to be what he wants them to be but to leave them continually free to become whatever they have it in them to become in the world he has created for them so that they may rise out of his creating heart and spirit with their own rich measure of his truth the way you and I rise out of God's heart and become forever part of it.

When Job, like Gloucester, cries out to God to enter his world and deliver him from the darkness that has befallen him, we know in detail just what that darkness is, but in his Second Letter to the Corinthians, Saint Paul, on the other hand, leaves his darkness for us to imagine. He speaks only of "the affliction we experienced in Asia," says only, "we were so utterly, unbearably crushed that we despaired of life itself." Who knows what affliction he is referring to, but at the same time who does not know well what it means to be afflicted like that? Who of us, looking back at our lives, cannot remember moments of such nearly unbearable sadness?

In my case, I have found that often such moments occur in conjunction with moments of nearly unbearable joy. Two years ago, for instance, I met the first of my grandchildren for the first time, and it was on a staircase that I met him. My daughter Dinah, his mother, was coming down carrying him in her arms, and I was going up with my heart in my mouth to meet him—this very small boy named Oliver with the blood in his veins of so many people I have loved, this fragile little bit of a two-month-old child who, God willing, will carry some fragment of who I am into a future I will never see. He was on his way down into the world, and I was on my way up out of it into God only knows what unimaginable world awaits every one of us if indeed any world beyond this one awaits us at all. On the one hand there was my joy at seeing him for the first time, which brought tears to my eyes, but on the other hand part of where those tears came from was the realization that the world he was entering was full of great sorrow as well as of great gladness, the realization that he will one day die even as I also will one day before I can ever know what becomes of him. That is a far cry from the anguish of Job and the despair of Paul—maybe only the saints are strong enough to look into the abyss—but it is of the same texture and substance, I think, and leads something deep in me to call out in Job's words, "Oh, that I knew where I might find him!" Oh, that we all of us knew where we might find the One who beyond any world we can imagine wipes every tear from our eyes and death from our hearts and creates all things new.

Job and Paul both found him before they were through although it was only Paul who knew him by name. God never answered Job's question as to why it is that bad things happen to good people and why, as Sir Walter Raleigh knew, those two narrow words, *hic jacet,* in the long run will cover us all, good and bad alike. But my guess is that it was not an answer that Job was really after, not some sort of theological explanation of the problem of suffering, which would have left him wiser than he was before but suffering still. I believe instead that what Job was really after was not God's answer but God's presence. And of course that was what Job finally found because the way God entered the world without destroying it was to enter Job's heart even as from the depths of his heart Job cried out to him. And that is the way he makes himself present to all of us.

In the greatest aria that God sings in the entire Bible, he sets forth in gorgeous poetry all the mystery and grandeur of creation as a way of showing Job that the mystery is ultimately unfathomable, and it is then that Job finally says, "I had heard of thee by the hearing of the ear, but now my eye sees thee" (42:5). And that was what Job needed above all else—not an explanation of suffering but the revelation that even in the midst of suffering there is a God who is with us and for us and will never let us go.

It was a few miles outside the city of Damascus that Paul made the same overwhelming discovery. He was on his way to bring back to Jerusalem for punishment members of the heretical sect who called themselves Christians when Christ himself appeared to him and called him by name and gave him a new faith to live for and die for, a faith that led him to write years later, "I am sure that neither death, nor life . . . nor things present, nor things to come . . . nor anything else in all creation, will be able to separate us from the love of God in Christ Jesus our Lord" (Romans 8:38–39).

So Job, the rich man, and Paul, the tent-maker, both of them in their darkest moments, found, or were found by, the light that shines in the darkness and that not even the darkness can ever finally overcome. And may it prove so, also, for you and for me, as I believe it proved so too for all the great ones lying in Westminster Abbey at whose names the world once trembled, as well as for all the others whose names have been all but forgotten. I believe that if their ghosts were to rise before us now and their long-stilled tongues able to speak once more, they would tell us with one voice of the unimaginable grace and mercy of God.

11

❖ ❖ ❖ ❖ ❖

The Gates of Dawn

When he drew near to Bethphage and Bethany, at the mount that is called Olivet, he sent two of the disciples, saying, "Go into the village opposite, where on entering you will find a colt tied, on which no one has ever yet sat; untie it and bring it here. If anyone asks you, 'Why are you untying it?' you shall say this, 'The Lord has need of it.'" So those who were sent went away and found it as he had told them. And as they were untying the colt, its owners said to them, "Why are you untying the colt?" And they said, "The Lord has need of it." And they brought it to Jesus, and throwing their garments on the colt they set Jesus upon it. And as he rode along, they spread their garments on the road.

As he was now drawing near, at the descent of the Mount of Olives, the whole multitude of the disciples began to rejoice and praise God with a loud voice for all the mighty works they had seen, saying, "Blessed is the King who comes in the name of the Lord! Peace in heaven and glory in the highest!" And some of the Pharisees in the multitude said to him, "Teacher, rebuke your disciples." He answered, "I tell you, if these were silent, the very stones would cry out."

And when he drew near and saw the city he wept over it, saying, "Would that even today you knew the things that make for peace! But now they are hid from your eyes. For the days shall come upon you, when your enemies will cast up a bank about you and surround you, and hem you in on every side, and dash you to the ground, you and your children within you, and they will not leave one stone upon another in you; because you did not know the time of your visitation."

Luke 19:29–44

One way of looking at Palm Sunday is as a kind of Last Hurrah. It wasn't like the Saint Patrick's Day parade making its way down Fifth Avenue with the stripe in the middle painted green and bands playing and flags flying and thousands standing along the curb to watch it go by. It wasn't a high-stepping white charger that Jesus rode—only a bandy-legged little unbroken beast with a few old coats thrown over its back for a saddle. And presumably there were only a relative few to watch him ride by on it, some of them fiery-eyed followers, disciples, believers, some of them enemies, some of them just people who happened to be there at the time and had nothing better to do than hang around to see what the shouting was all about.

But even so there was a festive air about it, a feeling of high expectancy and excitement. At least among the faithful there was a sense of history being made, a sense that the great day had arrived and Israel's ancient dream of a messiah was going to be realized at last. Some of them cut branches from the trees and spread them out in front of the little beast for a kind of poor man's red carpet, palm branches maybe, although the Gospels don't say that they were. Some of them got so carried away that they went as far as to take some of their outer clothes off and spread them in the dusty road too the way maybe even some of us, if we'd been there, might have been tempted to take off our blue blazers or our cashmere sweaters and spread them out there with everything else. They were carried away because they believed, as you and I believe, or at least some of the time believe, or wish we could believe, that the one who came clip-clopping his way toward the city was indeed the one they hailed him as being.

"Blessed is the King who comes in the name of the Lord!" is how they hailed him. That is who they believed he was. He was the anointed one that Israel had been waiting centuries for and waits for still. He was the holy one who would bring peace and justice to a world where, then as now, there was little peace and little justice. He was the blessed one who would heal the sick and restore sight to the blind and somehow make sense of life, which much of the time seems random and senseless. For as long as it lasted, it was a moment of something like triumph both for Jesus and for those who believed in him, and it must have been all but unthinkable, even among those who had reason to expect it, that in less than a week the one who came in the name of the Lord would be abandoned by virtually everybody including the ones closest to him and put to death in what even for its time was a uniquely cruel and sickening way.

In Dallas, Texas, in November of 1963 a man with a home movie camera took some footage of another parade of sorts, and we have all of us seen it replayed over and over again as we have also seen Palm Sunday replayed over and over again. The bare-headed young president sits in the back seat of an open car with his elegant young wife beside him and people lining the road cheering and waving as he drives by, and if you're like me, even as you watch it, knowing full well the terrible thing that is only moments away from happening, you can't help hoping against all hope and all reason that this time by some miracle it won't happen. The assassin with his rifle will miss his mark, or he will change his mind at the last minute and not fire, or the president's car will veer off the road just in time, and one way or another the world will be spared the aching sadness and sense of irreparable loss that no one who was alive at the time will ever forget.

And with Jesus, today, there is almost the same kind of crazy hope that maybe this time—somehow, somehow—Judas will be loyal, and Peter will be brave, and when Jesus is brought before Pilate with his eyes swollen shut and his nose broken, the crowds will choose him to be spared instead of Barabbas, and Pilate will sink to his knees before him, and all through Jerusalem Romans and Jews, rich people and beggars, pickpockets and priests will embrace one another and weep. And the cross won't have to happen. And the world will be saved without that death of all deaths that even after two thousand years the world has never forgotten. But not all our hoping can change the way history worked out, and, for reasons beyond our power to fathom, God did not change it either, and Jesus keeps riding along through the countryside toward the same appalling end because there is nothing we can do, just as there was nothing anybody could do then, to save him.

When the Pharisees heard the faithful hailing him as "Blessed" and "King," they were so outraged by what they took to be the blasphemy of it that they told Jesus to shut them up, and his answer was, "I tell you, if these were silent, the very stones would cry out." But what I think the stony reality of things did cry out, and cries out still if you listen with more than your ears, is that as full of beauty and hope and holiness as life is, there is, beneath the surface, a deep darkness that in less than a week not only engulfed Jesus but that threatens always to engulf us all.

Jesus does not weep often in the Gospels, although heaven knows he had good reason to, but as he rounds a bend in the road or rides up over the crest of a hill and suddenly sees the city of Jerusalem lying before him, his tears come, and it is that same darkness that is their cause. He does not, as you might expect, weep for himself. Instead he weeps for the city. "Would that even today you knew the things that make for peace," he says to it with his bare feet tucked under the belly of the foal. "For the days shall come upon you when your enemies will cast up a bank about you and surround you, and hem you in on every side, and dash you to the ground, you and your children within you, and they will not leave one stone upon another in you; because you did not know the time of your visitation."

He weeps not because he knows, as he often predicted, that Jerusalem is going to destroy him. He weeps because he knows that Jerusalem itself is going to be destroyed, and destroyed it indeed was only some forty years later, destroyed by the Romans as completely as a few centuries later still Rome, as the Caesars knew it, and as Jesus knew of it, was destroyed too.

It is Jerusalem that he weeps for, but who can believe that it is only for Jerusalem? Who can believe that he doesn't weep also for Rome, and for Hiroshima, for Dresden, for Coventry, for Saigon, for what's left of Sarajevo, of Mogadishu? And who can believe that he doesn't weep also for New York, for London, for Amsterdam, Calcutta, Palm Beach, because his tears, I think, are not only for the cities that down through the centuries have been destroyed by the darkness of war but also for the cities and towns and villages where the darkness is subtler and deeper than war and therefore in a way even more destructive. I think he weeps for every place on the face of this heartbreaking planet where children have no food to eat and no place to turn to, and the dispossessed turn to lawlessness and chaos, and the homeless sleep wrapped up in newspapers to keep out the cold. And I think he weeps too for the rich who have homes all over creation but often can find no true home inside themselves and who add to the world's pain, and to their own pain, less by any evil they do than by the good they don't do, the good they could do, maybe even dream of doing but somehow never quite get around to doing very well, for the poor and broken of the world. I think he weeps for all those who hunger and thirst after righteousness but don't know where it is to be found, or are afraid to find it, or don't even know that it is what they are hungering for maybe more than they hunger for anything else. There at the bend in the road he weeps, in other words, for all of us and for the self-destroying, world-destroying darkness that is part of all of us, and says to you and to me as he said to Jerusalem all those centuries ago, "Would that even today you knew the things that make for peace," if only for peace inside our own skins.

What are those things? My guess is that they are close to the same things that lead us to go to church on Palm Sunday morning. We go for lots of reasons, of course. We go out of habit; it is what we were brought up to do on Sundays and what the chances are our parents and grandparents did before us. We go out of a sense of duty, the way we give money to charity or visit a friend in the hospital or vote in elections. We go because we enjoy the lovely old service maybe and believe it is somehow good for us the way we believe that physical exercise is good for us or listening to classical music or giving up alcohol for Lent. But beneath all such reasons as that, I think that, more than we realize, we go to find shelter from the storm.

For all its great beauty, this is a stormy world we live in, and we all of us have been through storms in the past that were almost the end of us, and we all of us face storms still to come, including the one, for each of us, that will be the end indeed. So we go in *faith*— faith that to worship, to pray, to receive the bread and wine even when we really have no clear idea why we are doing it or why it is supposed to be so important, or maybe just to be silent together, is to draw near to a holiness and mystery that lie as far beyond the power of darkness to touch as they lie beyond our power to do more than reach out for as a child reaches out in the darkness for a hand to take hold of.

We are not saints. Much of the time our faith is weak and the God we have faith in seems far away if not absent altogether. But we go to church nonetheless in *hope*—hope that God is truly God even so, hope that God will mend us where we are broken, and forgive us where we have a hard time forgiving ourselves, and breathe into us new life when the lives we are living seem empty and increasingly diminished by age and in the last analysis doomed.

And we go also, I think, in something like *love*. When we return to our pews after receiving Communion, sometimes we watch the faces of others returning to theirs. Some of them are the faces of friends or family faces that we know better than any other faces in the world. Some of them are the faces of strangers or near strangers. Some of them are faces that our hearts go out to, and some of them are faces that seem to shut us out as for no good reason our hearts seem to shut them out. But to watch them as they come back up the aisle is at least from time to time, by God's grace, to see them all, friends and strangers alike, as human beings bound on the same fateful journey that we are bound on, full of all the same hopes and misgivings, the same longings and memories, the same fears about tomorrow and confusions about today that also fill us. And when such times come, it is possible as we watch them move past us, I think, to reach out to them in our hearts and to wish them enormously well as though even the strangers among them are as precious to us as the people we have known longest and loved best in all the world.

Faith, hope, love—I think those are the things that make for peace, and when Jesus says that we don't know them, what I believe he means is that we know *about* them well enough, just as the citizens of Jerusalem knew about them, but that we don't know them in the sense of their having become part of who we are. We know that in one form or another these are the things that make for peace, but especially when the world storms around us and within us and when darkness makes it very hard to have faith, to hope, to love, we are apt to know little real peace inside ourselves.

But then there is also something we know that the citizens of Jerusalem did *not* know as they spread their branches and their garments out in the road before him. They knew better than we do what happened on Palm Sunday because they were there in the flesh to take part in it. With their own eyes they watched the procession finally enter the gates of the city that even in their day was ancient and holy. And like us, many of them must have known in their secret hearts, as Jesus knew in his, the horror that was bound to take place all too soon what with both Roman authority and Jewish orthodoxy afraid of what a messianic uprising would cost them if they didn't crush it before it got out of hand. But what they did not know because it still lay in the future—and what you and I *do* know because it is at the very heart of our faith—was what was going to happen on the outskirts of the city just a week after the Sunday when Jesus entered it.

It happened in the night. There was no one to see it happen or to hear it happen. There was no one later that day who really understood what had happened—not even Mary Magdalen, who was the first to discover it, not even the disciples, who could hardly believe what she said she had discovered—and there has never been anyone to this day who has really understood it. It was light coming out of darkness like the sun rising out of the sea. It was stillness and unspeakable relief following in the wake of storm. It was hope rising up out of shuddering despair. It was life springing like a lily, like a rose, out of death.

I believe that to draw near to that life in whatever way we can, to reach out for and embrace and breathe deeply of that life as it draws near us, is to know at last the one thing of all things that makes for peace truly and always. And I believe that if never quite to *know*, because such knowledge is too wonderful for us, but in our heart of hearts to have faith, to trust, to hope against hope that not even death can put an end to that life is the one thing that changes Palm Sunday from a Last Hurrah on the eve of unspeakable loss and sorrow to the first great Hosanna at the gates of dawn.

12

◇　◇　◇　◇　◇

Faith

Somewhere along the line Paul Tillich said something to the effect that doubt is not the opposite of faith but an element of faith, in other words goes hand in hand with it. I have faith that there is an all-loving, all-powerful God in spite of the fact that I have no sure way of knowing that there is. Not knowing for sure means that maybe I am wrong. That is where doubt comes in. Many wise and good people have believed that there is no such God. Maybe they were right. There is much evidence to support them, most notably perhaps the perpetual presence of suffering in the world.

A great deal of that suffering—the Holocaust, for instance— can be explained by saying that God leaves human beings free to do unspeakable things to each other presumably because, if they are not free to do unspeakable things to each other, they are not truly free to love each other either or to love God, the great double commandment that is laid upon us before all others. And if they are not truly free, they are not truly human as God intended them to be. Such reasoning as that may make it possible to believe in God in spite of suffering. But what about forms of suffering that human beings cannot be held responsible for like certain forms of disease or disability, for instance? What about fires and floods that kill thousands? Maybe the explanation there is that God leaves the creation itself free either to run as it was created to run or to run amok, and that the doctrine of the Fall pertains not just to the human order but to the natural order as well. Maybe so, but maybe not so.

There are times when all our explanations ring false even as we make them. There are times when it is hard to see how any honest, intelligent person can look at the world without concluding, like Macbeth, that the whole show is a tale told by an idiot, full of sound and fury and signifying nothing. Many of us have faith in God and yet have doubts too, and in the long run perhaps it is just as well that we have them. At least doubts prove that we are in touch with reality, with the things that threaten faith as well as with the things that nourish it. If we are not in touch with reality, then our faith is apt to be blind, fragile, and irrelevant.

All of this has to do with intellectual doubt, the kind of doubt that arises out of the process of logical, rational thought. But there is also what might best be called existential doubt, the kind of doubt that involves not just our minds but our total being and arises out of our experience of existence itself. I think of Job saying, "Let the day perish wherein I was born. . . . Why is light given to him that is in misery, and life to the bitter in soul, who long for death, but it comes not?" I think of Jeremiah's "O Lord, thou hast deceived me. . . . I have become a laughingstock all the day." I think ultimately of Jesus on the cross uttering his terrible "Eloi, Eloi" of dereliction. Existential doubt is something you reach not by a process of reasoning but by looking into the abyss itself, and there are few who can do that without being devastated.

God reserves his deepest silence for his saints, someone has said, and maybe only the saints can survive existential doubt. As for myself, despite all the questions about the validity of faith that occasionally cross my *mind*, I have never felt in my *stomach* what it must be to confront utter meaninglessness because far beneath all my misgivings, there is always the assumption that, beyond my power to understand, all is well. My faith is not strong enough, all-encompassing enough, even to imagine the appalling alternative.

For most of us, I suspect, faith is apt to be limited like that, as limited as our capacity to doubt is limited. We read the Scriptures, we hear sermons, we receive the sacraments, and at least from time to time, one hopes, we are nourished by them. We are moved by the men and women we meet whose lives seem to reflect a deeper faith than our own and by the great works of music, painting, and literature that are the expressions of such faith. We are moved also by those precious moments when something holy seems to break through into our lives both to heal us and to summon us to pilgrimage. In short, we look at the world and conclude from what we find that, all evidence to the contrary notwithstanding, we will, like Pascal, place our wager on God. Our faith is that wager. It is not just an *intellectual* assent—words like "nourished" and "moved" suggest that it goes much deeper than that—but just as in our doubt we do not feel in our stomachs what it must be to confront utter meaninglessness, so in our faith we rarely if ever feel in our stomachs what it must be to confront unutterable and unquestionable holiness. If God reserves his deepest silence for his saints, then maybe it is for his saints too that he reserves the beatific vision. We can only hope that, this side of that vision, such faith as we have will be enough to keep us going, just as, through thick and thin, it has been enough to keep us going until now.

As for what lies ahead, we can take great heart from Saint Paul's words to the Corinthians that although now we see only through a glass darkly, there will come a day when we will see face to face and understand fully even as we are fully understood. It is the nature of faith to look beyond itself—and beyond the doubts that must always exist in tension with it if it is a living faith—to a time on the far side of time when the holy dream is at last revealed to be reality and all that we take now for reality glimmers like a dream. In the meanwhile, faith is the way we have of seeing while we have only the dark glass to see through.

13

◇ ◇ ◇ ◇ ◇

Hope

If preachers decide to preach about hope, let them preach out of what they themselves hope for.

They hope that the words of their sermons may bring some measure of understanding and wholeness to the hearts of the people who hear them and to their own hearts. They hope that the public prayers they pray may be answered, and they hope the same for their private prayers and for the prayers of their congregations.

They hope that the somewhat moth-eaten hymns, the somewhat less than munificent offerings, and the somewhat perfunctory exchange of the peace may all be somehow acceptable in the sight of the One in whose name they are offered. They hope that the sacrament of bread and wine may be more than just a pious exercise.

They hope that all those who come faithfully to church Sunday after Sunday may find at least as much to feed their spirits there as they would find staying at home with a good book or getting into the fresh air for some exercise. At the heart of all their hoping is the hope that God, whom all the shouting is about, really exists.

And at the heart of the heart is Christ—the hope that he really is what for years they have been saying he is. That he really conquered sin and death. That in him and through him we also stand a chance of conquering them. "If Christ has not been raised, your faith is futile and you are still in your sins," Saint Paul wrote to the Corinthians. "If for this life only we have hoped in Christ, we are of all people most to be pitied" (1 Corinthians 15:17, 19). If preachers are going to talk about hope, let them talk as honestly as Saint Paul did about hopelessness. Let them acknowledge the darkness and pitiableness of the human condition, including their own condition, into which hope brings a glimmer of light.

And let them talk with equal honesty about their own reasons for hoping—not just the official, doctrinal, biblical reasons, but the reasons rooted deep in their own day-by-day experience. They have hope that God exists because from time to time they have been touched by God. Let them speak of those times with the candor and concreteness and passion without which all the homiletical eloquence and technique in the world are worth little.

They believe that Jesus is the resurrection and the life because at a few precious moments that is what they have found him to be in their own small deaths and resurrections. Let them speak of those moments not like essayists or propagandists but like human beings speaking their hearts to their dearest friends who at any given point will unerringly know whether they are speaking truth or only parroting it.

The trouble with many sermons is not so much that the preachers are out of touch with what is going on in the world or in books or in theology but that they are out of touch with what is going on in their own lives and in the lives of the people they are preaching to. Whether their subject is hope or faith or charity, let them speak out of the living truth of their own experience of those high matters. Let them have the courage to be themselves.

14

◇ ◇ ◇ ◇ ◇

Grace

At the start of virtually every one of his letters, grace is what Saint Paul wishes his friends first, even before mercy, even before peace, and no matter how much of a hurry he is in to get on with the main business of the letter, he always points out that this grace he wishes them is "from God our Father and the Lord Jesus Christ" because he wants there to be absolutely no doubt about that. Grace is the best he can wish them because grace is the best he himself ever received.

He was on his way to Damascus when he received it, of course. His mission was to round up as many followers of Christ as he could lay his hands on in order to bring them in chains back to Jerusalem, and it was precisely on his way to accomplish that mission that Christ appeared to him in a vision and asked him to become a follower himself. When it seemed to him that he deserved nothing so much as to have God give him up, God in Christ gave him himself instead, and Paul never forgot it his whole life long.

"By grace we are saved," he wrote, because he believed that, with no questions asked, no conditions laid down, no qualifications required, no strings of any kind attached, God had loved him enough to save him—*him* of all people—and from that day forward every word he ever wrote and every weary mile he ever traveled sprang from his passion to touch the heart of the world as his own heart had been touched by the revelation of that extraordinary moment.

There are all sorts of ways you can think about grace. You can think about it theologically and see *faith* as the way we welcome it with open arms into our lives. You can see *good works* as the fruit of welcoming it and of allowing our lives to be transformed by it rather than as the means of somehow earning it. You can think about it *biblically* and see Abraham and Sarah, David and Rahab as men and women whom God chose for his own not because they were Eagle Scouts and had it as their just due but simply because, by grace, he loved them warts and all and wanted them on his side. You can think about it *historically* and remember how Luther rediscovered it in the sixteenth century and changed the whole course of Western history by crying it from the rooftops of Wittenberg.

But when it comes to the mystery and beauty and power of grace in and of itself, you can do no better than to think about the only case of how it works in the human heart that you know intimately and personally, from the inside, and that is, of course, your own case. The chances are you would not be in any very meaningful sense a Christian at all unless at certain moments in your life you had been somehow overwhelmed by it on your way, if not to Damascus, then to wherever it was you happened to be going at the time. To love and seek to serve God other than just dutifully, uninspiredly, means that maybe not at one incandescent moment in your life, but in the course of many no more than dimly seen but holy moments, you were impassioned to do so.

We all have such moments to point to, but how easily they get lost in the random clutter and busyness of things. How much preaching we hear from the lips of men and women who give us no way of knowing that they were themselves once upon a time passionately moved by the gospel, which they proclaim now with so little apparent passion. Let them preach about the moments of grace in their own lives. Let them preach about the flesh-and-blood reality of those moments and about how, even though there are many other moments when grace seems faint and far away, those moments of grace remain their richest treasure and dearest hope.

Or if for some reason they shy away from preaching *about* those moments—either because they seem too precious or perhaps too threadbare and elusive to tell—then at least let them preach *out of* them because not to speak from the heart of where their faith comes from is to risk never really touching the hearts of those of us who so hungrily listen.

15

◇ ◇ ◇ ◇ ◇

Jesus

There is the Jesus Who Was, and there is the Jesus Who Is.

The Jesus Who Was is that fathomless, elusive, unpredictable, haunting, and finally unknowable figure who moves though the homely landscapes of the Synoptics and the twilit dreamscapes of John like a figure in an old newsreel. The film is scratched and faded. Some patches are almost blindingly light-struck and others all but totally dark. The sound track crackles and now and then cuts out or gives signs of having been dubbed. The editing is erratic. Yet for just that reason we treasure all the more each flickering glimpse of him that we are given as he stops at a well for water, or lies asleep in the stern of a boat with a pillow under his head, or tells his strange, off-beat stories to the people who have gathered to gawk at him.

We all have the Gospel moments that mean the most to us. As for me, I have always particularly treasured that moment when Pilate asks him, "What is truth?" and he stands there in silence, presumably because nothing he might possibly answer could be as eloquent as just his standing there. I treasure the moment on the cross when the good thief turns to him and, speaking for all of us, says, "Jesus, remember me"; and we know as surely as we know anything that Jesus remembers him and will always remember him. And the moment, after the resurrection, when just at dawn, on the beach, he is waiting by a charcoal fire and calls out to his fishermen friends, "Come and have breakfast." And in that first, fresh light, they come and have it. And have it from his hands. Have it from him. *Breakfast,* of all things!

The danger is that we hold on only to the moments that one way or another heal us and bless us and neglect the others. I think of his cursing the fig tree for not bearing fruit out of season and telling the Canaanite woman who came to him for help that it was not fair to take the children's food and throw it to the dogs. I think of his saying, "I was thirsty and you gave me no drink, I was a stranger and you did not welcome me, naked and you did not clothe me," and of his terrible question, "Are you able to drink the cup that I am to drink?" and of his terrible warning, "Woe to you, when all men speak well of you, for so their fathers did to false prophets." Woe to all of us if we stay only in the bright uplands of the Gospels and avoid like death, avoid like life, the dark ravines, the cave under the hill.

It is the Jesus Who Was who said, "Come to me, all who labor and are heavy laden, and I will give you rest," and it is the Jesus Who Is who says it now—he unto whom all hearts are open, all desires known, and from whom no secrets are hid—and says it almost unbearably to every last one of us, the young as well as the old, the lucky as well as the unlucky, the victimizer as well as the victim, because there is not one of us who is not in some way heavy laden and in need of what he brings. Perhaps it is by what he brings that we know best the Jesus Who Is. To the blinded he brings vision. To the deafened the sound of a voice unlike all other voices. To the deadened the breath of life. *Rest*.

The Jesus Who Is is the one whom we search for even when we do not know that we are searching and hide from even when we do not know that we are hiding. "Come, Lord Jesus" is the way the Bible ends, and it is as The One Who Comes that we know him most truly. Perhaps no one has described it more movingly than Albert Schweitzer:

> He comes to us as One unknown, without a name, as of old, by the lakeside, He came to those who knew Him not. He speaks to us the same word: "Follow thou me!" and sets us to the tasks which He has to fulfil for our time. He commands. And to those who obey Him, whether they be wise or simple, He will reveal Himself in the toils, the conflicts, the sufferings which they shall pass through in His fellowship, and, as an ineffable mystery, they shall learn in their own experience Who He is.
>
> A. Schweitzer, *The Quest of the Historical Jesus*,
> trans. W. Montgomery (London: A. and C. Black, 1922), p. 401.